Catherine Brunelle, B.Sc., PA LEED®

Ecological Love:
The Theory

Translated from French (Canada)
by Francine Mayer

Essay

Ecological Love Editions

«*Mona*» by *Hélène Blais,* painter, *1985*

Cover page illustration: "Mona", Acrylique 24" x 36", by *Hélène Blais*, painter, 1985

http:/heleneblais.blogspot.com

Back cover photograph: Studio de Lottinville Granby, Québec, Canada. © 2013

www.EcologicalLove.com

E-mail: info@EcologicalLove.com

First Edition: Third Quarter 2015

Legal Deposit – Bibliothèque et Archives Nationales du Québec, Third Quarter, 2015 – Library and Archives Canada, Third Quarter, 2015.

ISBN : 978-2-924497-00-5

CONTENTS

Part Three: *POSITIONING*

Part Four: *IMPLICATIONS*

Part Five: COMMITMENT

Dedication

To all the people I have the good fortune to love, my dear family, my friends, and to all the people on Earth, for the constant joy they make me feel, but also, for the people who live in poverty, and for which I feel tremendous compassion.

I do what I want and what I can with my life, and I am learning more and more how to respect my choices and my desires as they are the reflection of natural beauty.

This book intentionally grew out of the science of sociology and the author's subjective point of view.

Catherine Brunelle, B.Sc., PA LEED®
Sociologist and lecturer

Note to Readers

Ecology is the study of living beings in their environment and the interactions between them. Everything today bears the stamp of ecology. It is therefore logical to talk about *Ecological Love*. But what is the difference between *Ecological Love* and the usual ways we think about love?

Is the way we experience kinship relations purely personal or do we learn how to behave with others according to specific models? Do the proposed models influence our actions; do they represent responsible behaviours that will have a greater impact on the ecosystem?

Do intimate human relationships contribute to environmental balance, in harmony with material resources and the well-being of individuals? What are the characteristics of a love lived in freedom, the faith we place in it, and the positive effects it has on the ecosystem, including living conditions?

The *Ecological Love* concept is based on a sociological analysis from a humanistic approach, from the great years of global feminism until today, using a method and a scientific framework in the search for truth and freedom, and which has given birth, among others, to a revolutionary movement about the genders in the last third of the previous century.

Let us recall who the opposing forces are: the sovereign people, the church's authority and its discourse, namely the duty to increase the population, with its unique advantages and immense pleasures, but also the distress that comes with this obligation; unbridled increase in population, poverty and the social changes that this implies.

At the heart of the great systems of thought

lies the duty to increase populations; this requires individuals to enter into a relationship with one other person of the opposite sex, for the sole purpose of starting a family.

In these dictatorial systems – where coercion and terror are used to force people to obey – relationships solely aimed at reproduction are the only ones accepted. It is precisely this basic premise of forced reproduction that gives rise to horrific abuses, like homophobic laws, which in turn have a great bearing on the humanist spirit, more open and more sensitive to the differences and the will of others

In reality, there are not two, but three genders: female, male and intersex persons. Yet, in the case of "gender", it is dreadful to note the arbitrary nature of the assignation of gender roles, whose sole duality diminishes any possibility that might recognize the existence of more than two genders. This important fact opens the way to serious aberrations like the concept of homophobia, a pure creation of dictatorial minds to better serve their own interests, at the expense of seeking the well-being of humans forcibly subjected to this system.

This book intentionally grew out of the science of sociology and the author's subjective point of view. Its ultimate aim is to acknowledge as legitimate, free, healthy and ecological relationships, in contrast to relationships, where too often people are subjected to coercion and poverty.

Introduction

The emancipation of human beings, human power and its applications are the main topics of my on-going research. The issue is to demonstrate how effectively we can achieve changes in our respective lives and in a given society, in light of the tremendous strides achieved by the humanist movement with its particular focus on Global Feminism and its effects. Indeed, since 1975, year designated by the UN as "International Women's Year", a wealth of research has been used to identify and rectify uncomfortable human situations, such as those related to gender. Numerous achievements were made such as exercising control over our bodies through the holistic self-health movement and with plants and other tangible or intangible elements found in nature. This resulted, amongst other things, in the extraordinary recognition of the field of natural medicine around the world and in the creation of informative archives from a variety of international sources namely on the healing powers of medicinal plants and other natural remedies.

The extensive study of sensuality, sexuality and genitality has enabled us to recognize the abusive material contained in the – oh so restrictive – binary distinction between genders. We have also learned that supporting information about love, in a way that advocates exclusively heterogeneity of relations, tends to inevitably subjugate people to reproductive, fertilization, gestation and birthing processes.

As such, the aspect of cooperation or simply associating oneself with a view to improving living conditions can be completely removed from certain processes in favour of procreation alone, and on a broader level, the organization of the family.

In light of these concerns, and more importantly, since 1975, societies have greatly evolved regarding, among other things, the financial independence of individuals from the point of view of their physical, psychological, emotional and spiritual independence.

A great number of us, citizens of the Earth, are born to parents who were obliged to procreate, and at times we were not breastfed because post-war mothers had been forced to prefer giving their babies formula milk instead of their own milk, in response to suggestions made by institutionalized medicine and the pharmaceutical industry.

I will mention in particular, several testimonials who speak out on behalf of reproductive freedom and the coercive mechanisms who threaten it, while being confident that a worldwide debate will soon take place on this issue.

This book is the result of a deep commitment and a rigorous dedication towards the experience of supreme justice in the world. My research is based essentially on sociological information obtained from a variety of empirical sources and narrative testimonies recorded during special meetings from 1973 to today, at formal and informal, local, provincial, national, international and global conferences on human rights, etc., namely the *United Nations Fourth World Conference on Women* and its NGO Forum held in Beijing, China, in 1995 and the well-known *Women's Music Festival*, We Want the Music Collective (WWMC), held every year for nearly four decades in Michigan, USA, as well as those held in Quebec, Canada, France, Italy and the United States, in which I took and active part.

I attended a great number of meetings in many countries which focused primarily on the two broad themes of poverty and violence.

During these citizen meetings held during the important years when sexist models were being shattered, each participant was asked to speak freely, almost always through an open procedure advocating the natural order of communication, and in which no one was assigned a specific speaking time and there mostly was no mediation. During the discussions, we had a great opportunity to share magical moments about problems that emerged in our childhood, our adolescence and our adult lives, and were characterized among other things, by an unrestrained sexuality, intriguing and inadequate to say the least, and where a more global view of sexuality was loudly called into question.

Ecological Love: The Theory reports the results of an enormous amount of work accomplished over a thirty-five year period when tremendous and significant efforts were being made to highlight the creation of sustainable mechanisms for peace and for the well-being of the population worldwide.

This book neither advocates nor offers, but reveals vigorously and candidly in such a way that tends to clarify and simplify the rudiments of a practice, which although widespread, remains very much in the background. While claiming to participate in the fine-tuning of human relationships, this overview aims at promoting a very modest position in a world where a more insensitive genitality wants to occupy all the space as a distorted symbol of postmodern sensuality.

Throughout its pages, *Ecological Love* wants to convey the desire of sharing the beauty and greatness of a respectful and caring love. It emphasizes and recognizes the passion that supporters of such an essential love have and which focuses primarily on ultra consciousness motivated by super-dynamic convictions.

This book is not meant to be controversial, but is the perfect opportunity to present a brilliant alternative to conventional love, that is, well sometimes unimaginable – and even alarming – while pretending to be unobtrusively compulsory.

We have to admit that many people feel imprisoned in a sexual straightjacket that literally poisons their existence because of its complexity and often disastrous consequences. How many teens today are directed towards practices which appear to be more traditional and which they embrace, albeit reluctantly, because of a lack of healthier alternatives?

One only has to look at the tragic statistics on sexually transmitted diseases and look closely at human scandals – poverty is central to this – to realize how someone, somewhere is not doing a very good job. So there you have it!

This sad statement inevitably leads us to question ourselves on the importance of empowerment with respect actions taken and their actual impact on the development of human life.

This book humbly offers a healthier and more ecological approach to the sometimes complicated choices we all face regarding relationships and communications.

Following the emergence of a more humane way of thinking, a clear stance and a strong personal and social commitment, this approach is integrated into a more natural economic advancement movement geared to improving the living conditions of the Earth's citizens and is completely supported by the theory of *Ecological Love*.

Part One: *CONTEXT*

Chapter 1

Gender Polarization

Far be it for me to ignore the fact that many of us seem perfectly at ease in polarized gender roles where one elegantly portrays women's qualities and the other reflects, quite energetically I might add, masculine values and looks.

However, one should consider the fact that some human beings choose a different life path. They are healthy and authentic, sometimes they are intersex, or they just simply love the clothes, the ways and the attitudes that are exclusively reserved for the opposite gender, but whatever path they choose will often lead to serious consequences that are largely unfounded.

Numerous studies have shown that from birth, little human beings are being stigmatized as a result of their belonging to a gender that must absolutely be stereotyped.

The differences between female "F" and male "M" characters we see in magazines, films, and in reality, are often shown with very little details like looks, hairdo and clothes, amongst other things. However, in order for each human being to conform, terrible punishments often disguised as threats are made, and cast doubts as to the purity of the intentions underlying such strong humanophobic reactions and so much misanthropy.

Dresses, shoes, and hairdo are only theatre accessories! Hopefully we all agree that they in no way represent the serious and distinctive elements which are part of the actual gender of a person.

However, in modern societies we note the excessive importance given when identifying a person according to those specific criteria, thus categorizing him or her...all the while believing we are not wrong about this.

Also, these models vary in practice. For instance, how do you differentiate between genders when one is wearing sports or work clothes and when customary criteria are scarce and distinctions are blurred? How do you identify each person's gender in eastern and western cities and countrysides when clothing is identical, or so similar, and friendship is visible between interchangeably intermixed genders?

During the key years of international feminism, we analysed in great details the characteristics linked to genders. What a year it was when we discovered how a proposed model, intended to be typically feminine, contributed, oddly enough, to the reduction of mobility and self assurance! Fitted dresses with plunging neckline, hair piled up high, lots of make-up, stiletto heels... and in some cultures this disguise served as a model to supposedly measure a person's femininity. However, experience, life and analysis have prompted us to identify *the inherent characteristics linked to gender,* based on the characteristics of the genital organs of a person rather than by using superficial or random characteristics such as criteria based only on clothes, looks or hairdo; elements we can rightfully consider as being totally unnecessary.

Moreover, this duality is quite superfluous. In a situation where reality is important, we should recognize the actual existence of three genders instead of two: females "f", males "m" and intersex "i" – also called hermaphrodites? –.

"According to the Organization Intersex International, 17 people out of 1000 are born with genital organs difficult or impossible to identify as being male or female." (Cf. Société, Naître avec les deux sexes, chercher son identité, http://ici.radio-canada.ca/emissions/medium_large/2014-2015/chronique.asp?idChronique=356387) *(in French only)*

But who needs to know if you belong to one gender or the other and who finds it so important to suppress the 3rd alternative so that intersex individuals must choose between two solutions – sometimes with great difficulty – especially when either gender corresponds to their innermost being? Who is interested in making sure there are only 2 identities instead of 3? Are they the same people whose interest it is to establish there is only one way to mix the genders, the “f” type with the “m” type?

In the science of probabilities, reality shows us that there are 6 possible ways: “f/f” “f/m”, “f/i”, “m/m”, “m/i” and “i/i”. Is there a dictatorship in place who wants to reduce human life to an “f/m” type? Well, there is every reason to believe it. There is indeed evidence showing that obeying this diktat has a direct corollary to considering the other five situations as being “deviant”. And, when the axe falls, such a severe judgement has tremendous repercussions on the persons concerned.

In the sixties for example, a brilliant student in obstetrics was denied her diploma when a letter she had written to a friend was callously intercepted by authorities, and in which she said “*...the long night we spent together in Quebec City...*” This young woman from Gaspé was ostracized in her 20’s and severely punished simply because she walked through the streets in Old Quebec with a friend and allegedly had a “homosexual” relationship. Without any evidence, she was demoted and asked to see a psychologist due to her deviant behaviour. Disoriented and deprived of a respectable career, her life was ruined; her calling, her determination to study and her brilliant performances, all were unjustly denied to her. All of this came about because of a prohibited human friendship... and it was shocking to say the least.

Yet, this singular and cruel incident where someone’s freedom is limited, happens very often, and is still happening on many different occasions and in many countries.

Every day, in a number of countries around the world, totalitarian leaders shamelessly establish laws aimed at torturing people who are against their diktat...

From a humanistic perspective, we can surely qualify the morality of these people, these heads of states or institutions as being suspicious, particularly when they declare that “non-reproductive” sexual relationships are “unnatural”. This is decidedly irreverent and intrudes in the intimate and personal life of their compatriots!

Chapter 2

Humanophobia

These absurd views have peaked my curiosity as to what the motivations are behind such barbaric and virulent behaviours toward social phenomena – friendship and affection between people – regarding simple human traits, and deserving of our deepest respect, even between same-sex people.

Just think of all we can accomplish when freedom of association and alliance prevails...Is this fundamental right at risk in today's world? How, for whom and why should friendship between same-sex people be threatening?

In fact, each human being has a more or less fifty-fifty chance to form a friendship with a person of the same sex. When they reach adolescence, many are saddened by having to force themselves into an inevitable denial because they are so overcome by the fear of being rejected or exterminated outright solely on the basis of having pure friendly encounters with same-sex people. What a cruel outcome for someone at such a young age, to be deprived of the power of tenderness!

What is this relentless manipulation that comes from an ancient or more recent past, has no foundation or relevance and absolutely horrendous outcomes? There must surely be a common thread to explain the existence of such inhumanity when two same-sex people are involved.

According to my research, the only logical response that explains this is the presence of a dogma around compulsory human reproduction, a form of tyranny in which people are forced to mate in order to reproduce, even against their wishes.

As such, many firmly attest to the veracity of this reality. Between 1945 and 1967, and particularly in Quebec, a number of influential people used threats such as excommunication or burning in hell, among other things, to force young religious youth to engage in specific intimate behaviours – as is abundantly described in numerous stories – thus repressing individual freedoms. It is the expression of an absolutely horrible repressive power established by delusional, insane and pervert boors and their no less despicable representants who endlessly promote these views.

These prescribed behaviours require all persons to engage in intimate interpersonal relationships for reproductive purposes only. The instructions are quite clear: there will be no feelings of sensuality either in friendship or in pleasurable relationships.

In fact, enormous pressure is applied so that pleasurable feelings are inevitably geared towards conception. To do so, certain guidelines must be strictly followed: the most important of which, according to the logic of mating for reproductive purposes, is to unite together only female and male types.

With the terrible goal to cut people off from their own life and sensual pleasures, let us remember what happened in the forties, fifties and sixties, in Quebec, when senseless and absurd rules were put into place in order to take away a person's right to feel sensual pleasure.

And frankly, you will certainly agree, only a senseless fool would believe he has the power to prevent a person from feeling pleasure. Nevertheless, it was happening in our part of the world. Numerous women believing they had to follow the diktat, took cold showers to diminish their feelings of pleasure. However, upon reflection, even if a person is indoctrinated, and despite any attempts to do so, she cannot ignore the "feelings" in her body, they are the essence of being. And sensual pleasure is the very essence of pleasure.

Pleasure – with its degrees, ranges and infinite variations – is a very important guide for making decisions and taking action. Just to think of cutting people off from their right to feel pleasure is absolutely evil and shows complete ignorance of human biology, suggesting the authors of such a belief have deep psychopathic traits.

"Ecological Love" argues that there is a correlation between social problems and dictatorship. The utmost vicious diktat, the obligation to develop human relationships centered on reproduction, is the greatest deception of all times reaching unsurpassed levels of implementation.

This state of affairs leads to extreme and cruel poverty, and is intolerable amongst world populations. This diktat forbids people in many countries to live a pure and simple love; horrendous violence is heinously orchestrated and perpetrated against same-sex lovers.

And it would seem that the activities of this fanatical dictatorship have increased since the Second World War, which no doubt served as a stepping stone to terrorize vulnerable populations.

It follows, then, that our sexual activities seem to remain linked to a sexuality modelled extensively after this imposed model. And this opens the way for children to procreate children, who procreate children and so on, thus carefully perpetuating the duty to reproduce – whether in agreement or against their will – and each child, once grown up, will tirelessly, and without a doubt carve herself or himself a decent place, using ingenious ways, in a conquered world where excesses will have wreaked its havoc: our numbers have dramatically increased only in the last two hundred years.

Chapter 3

Demography

The following United Nations chart shows the dramatic

Figure 1: Evolution of World Population over the last Two Thousand Years

In billions

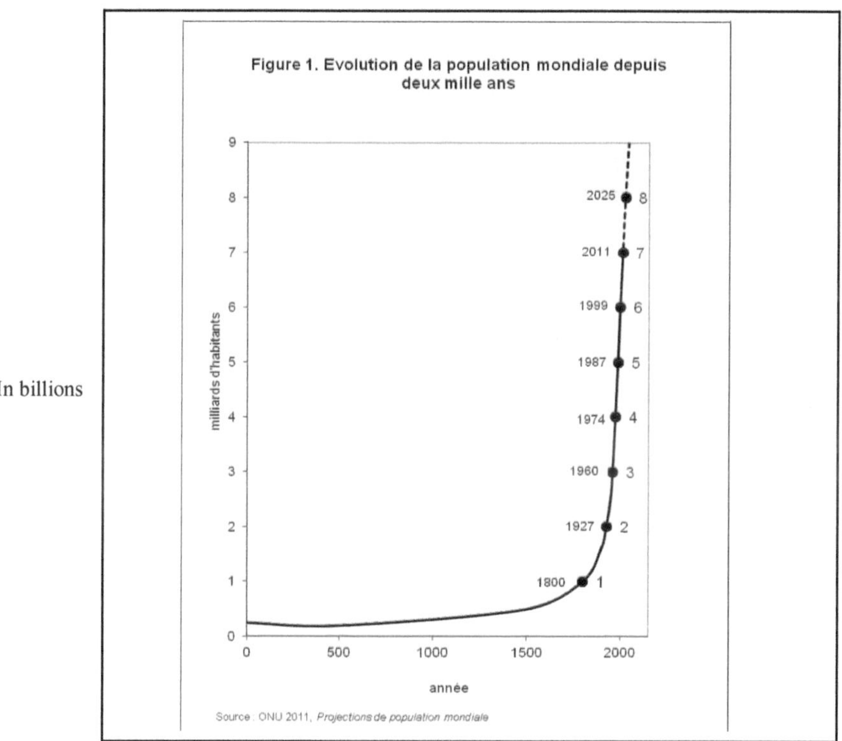

rise in the evolving curve of the world's population from year 0 of our era.*(Cf.*http://encyclopedie-dd.org*/encyclopedie/terre/les-perspectives-demographiques.html)(in French only)*. It's as if, in 1800, with the arrival of technological developments and the possibilities for industrial growth, some people had anticipated what it would be like to have access to an exponential increase in revenues – using human beings as pawns – exploiting workers and paying them low wages, to the detriment of the majority, in an ever increasing over-population context. It's as if mathematics, using only basis calculations, led people to expect record breaking profits in the event of a growth in population.

Thus, sometimes in densely populated areas, those deprived of the basic necessities become easy targets for massive and reckless hiring practices.

Of course, it's the responsibility of each person to be aware that his or her actions, even the most intimate ones have consequences. So when facing political or social pressure, especially from our loved ones, there is no doubt we will choose the least dangerous behaviours and tend to act according to more socially acceptable values.

Education is very important when people are in the process of choosing behaviours. Although everyone receives the same education they won't necessarily behave in the same way. However, a strict and rigorous education leaves little room for freedom of action. While appearances do not always indicate it, this is how it is in love relationships. The instructions are clear, and if they are not obeyed, you automatically put yourself in a dangerous situation. “Mate and procreate” is the most widespread rule of life in the world at this time.

In more liberated countries, however, a new trend is emerging concerning pressures to engage in procreation. A broad movement is taking place in the area of personal decisions, namely on the control of one's own reproduction – even sometimes not to reproduce at all – despite the opposition from different schools of thought including overcautious economists who tend to advocate rather thoughtlessly an increase in birth rate using – hogwash – the enormous national debt repayment, etc...

Many scientists, demographers, economists, sociologists, and others, as well as a significant part of the general population agree that free and informed reproduction in a society ensures a more natural fluctuation of the population, allowing for better social integration and encourages the emergence of the financial health of all its citizens.

Also, the intentions of the various political stakeholders could be at best, the well-being of the population, or at worst, could be based on specific economic indicators serving only the interests of a tiny portion of individuals.

For example, in order to increase automotive sales a company would be inclined to strongly support an increase in the number of consumers.

However, in order to improve living conditions, we need to consider per capita income, encourage policies that facilitate access to capital and offer loans that specifically target small and medium-size companies.

It is also acceptable to promote the idea that individuals make informed decisions based on their ability to manage their own lives and that of their offsprings as well. In which case, we encourage natural reproductive freedom in ecological and loving relationships, where living conditions ensure adequate care for potential genitors and their offsprings if any.

And in a context where real freedom of association exists, what would be a natural birth rate? Certainly one better suited to access available wealth and quality resources...Thank you!

Two opposing forces are at work here. On the one hand, the existence of extremely coercive measures targeting excessive human reproduction, and on the other, a widespread movement empowering each person who embraces *Ecological Love*, purely and simply.

What a great temptation it is to promote compulsory mating within a central authority, for example, and a political system where leaders calculate taxes and fees and estimates – with great interest – the surpluses generated by an eventual increase in the number of their subjects!!

According to the following reference, *(Cf.*http://fr.wikipedia.org/wiki/Population_mondiale*)*(in French only), it is estimated that since the dawn of times demography looks something like this:

Year	World Population
-100000	0.5 million
-10000	1 to 10 million
-6500	5 to 10 million
-5000	5 to 20 million
400	190 to 206 million
1000	254 to 345 million
1250	400 to 416 million
1500	425 to 540 million
1700	600 to 679 million
1750	629 to 691 million
1800	0.813 to 1.125 billion
1850	1.128 to 1.402 billion
1900	1.550 to 1.762 billion

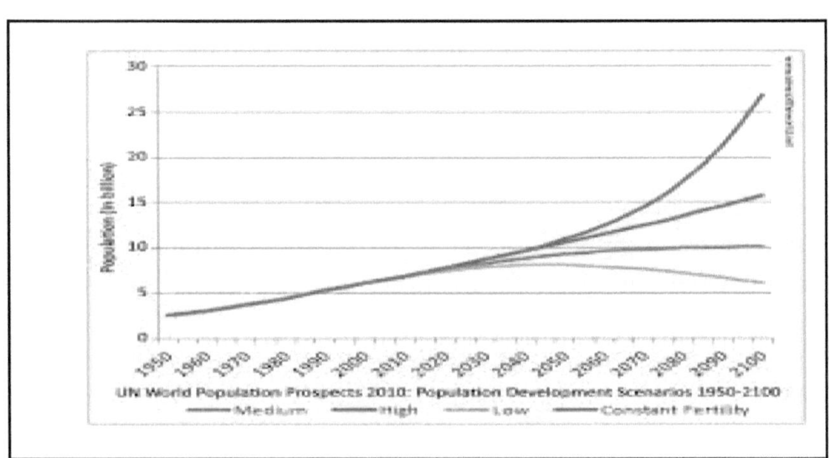

UN Chart, 2013

(see http://eng.wikipedia.org/wiki/World_Population*)*

Contrary to several estimates that did not take into account the power of individuals to counter the demographic growth, the above chart – World Population Projections, published by the United Nations in the spring of 2013 – takes into consideration possible fluctuations in demographic growth. Three different scenarios were thus developed based on high, medium and low fertility rates. According to future fertility rates, world population will be respectively 15.8 billion, 10.1 billion and 6.2 billion by the year 2100. For reference purposes, if the fertility rate remains at its present level, world population will have reached almost 27 billion by the year 2100.

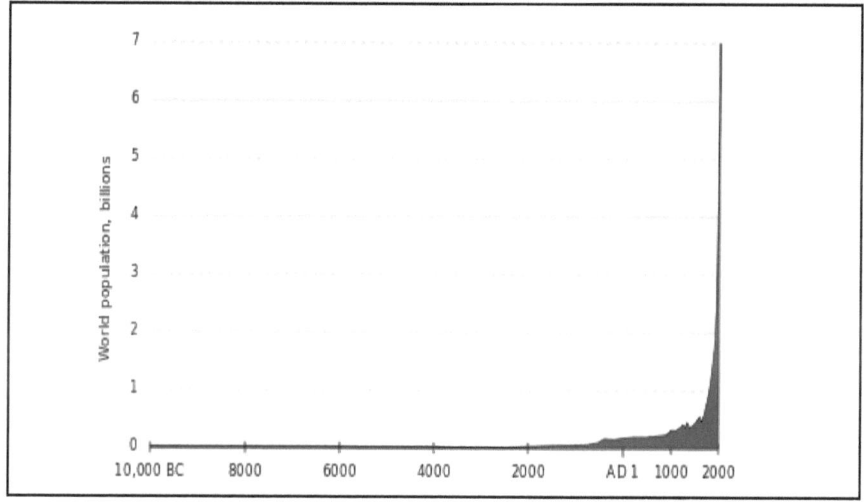

(Cf. A compilation of an increase in birth rates over time. http://fr.wikipedia.org/wiki/Population_mondiale)

Global population growth between 10000 BC and 2000

It is estimated that in the year 0, there were 170 million inhabitants in the world.

Between 540 and 770, the plague killed 100 million inhabitants. During this period the population remained stable at 190 million inhabitants.

In the year 1000, the population reached 310 million inhabitants.

In 1500, the population reached 425 million inhabitants.

In 1815, the population reached 1000 million inhabitants.

Up until 1815, the population increased by up to 4 million inhabitants a year. (Large numbers of child deaths + life expectancy of less than 40 years.)

Wars and pandemics had fewer negative impacts on global demographic growth.

In 1850 (industrial revolution)	1,260 million
In 1900	1,650 million
In 1927	2,000 million
In 1960	3,000 million
In 1974	4,000 million
In 1987	5,000 million
In 2011	7, 000 million

The most dramatic rise occurring in the XIX century, when we began to see attempts by the pharmaceutical and food industry, even the telecommunications, general transport, computer industries or others, to promote the growth of human numbers. Actually, these attempts are very real and very obvious: the general population is under a great deal of pressure to increase, without reservation and shamelessly, the demographic index of certain populations and of the general population as well.

The primary tools used abundantly by multiple authorities, is to try and limit the freedom of association by imposing the "f/m" model where copulation occurs as a matter of course. And with it, on the political scene of every continent of the world, comes a strong opposition against the *union* of same-sex couples. If the desire to force people to copulate using the "f/m" model did not exist, there would be no deep obsession to repress same-sex friendship, sensitivity, sensuality or even tenderness with such vigor and determination!

What are the reasons for such violence on the part of authorities against same-sex people having closer ties? How legitimate is this school of thought when an alliance is formed between one or more churches? At a time when ecological upheavals due to overpopulation, and the depletion processes of soils and oceans, which has already started, one can rightly question the kinds of actions that should be taken to urgently address the incongruity of such formidable attacks on the part of these authorities.

Part Two: *BIASED SEXUALITY*

Chapter 4

Guidelines

What happens in situations when two persons of the same sex do not really commit acts that can be defined as genital sex? For example, who would dare claim that same-sex couples who hold each other by the waist must inevitably lead to inappropriate sexual behaviour? Which of those behaviours are considered to be criminal by the powers that be? And how do they describe them? Where do you draw the line between tenderness and pleasure? And who gets to set the guidelines?

And if, for example, an intersex person loves another intersex person, by what standards will they be judged? This is a major issue! What if they don't consider themselves as belonging to either of the other two genders? Unless they each choose to belong to one of the other two acceptable...different genders, even if it means switching roles from time to time. As a social proposal, how twisted is that!

> *Cf. Fraternal kiss between Brejnev (URSS) and Honecker (GDR- East Germany), taken in 1979 by French photographer Régis Bossu on the 30th anniversary of the GDR.*

It is indeed quite a fraternal kiss! How magnificent this display of affection in the name of peace! Why are we not able to express this kind of affection in Russia these days? How can a country prevent people from simply meeting and showing this type of affection? It's a darn shame! On one hand, it is forbidden to hold each other and on the other, penetration and ejaculation into someone else's cavity is imposed!!! Isn't this quite incongruous?

It seems to me that a more honest question to ask is not "with whom" do we do things, but "what it is we do", in terms of intimate acts? This is a much more important issue. Also, why automatically pretend people view intimacy in the same way? Who decides what the truth is? A dictatorship that imposes gender normalcy as well as sexual acts geared towards reproduction? Hence, even though you may not wish to reproduce, the reproductive gestures seem so inevitable you have to resort to a birth control subterfuge. Doesn't that seem to be a very underhanded way to indoctrinate?

As well, when people believe contraceptives are linked to sexual freedom, are they totally wrong!! Also, the energy it took for us to question everything during the women's movement has taught us to reclaim our sexual pleasure simply, without artifice nor trickery, without detours nor escapes without shortcuts nor excuses, without deception, nor ploy, and to stay outside the contraception/conception realm, but within an exceptional context where desire, joy and tenderness are its main ingredients!

This is so very obvious: prescribed sexual acts – including conception (penetration and ejaculation into an orifice) – are proving to be highly inadequate at the present time. Health Canada claims that between 70% and 80% of sexually active individuals will contract "sexual" diseases. Undoubtedly, with such a high incidence of infections, it is obvious that the relationship model most people adopt is quite inappropriate!

The question that immediately comes to mind is the criteria used by Health Canada to determine sexual activity. In literature, the reproductive pattern is everywhere: this activity is "recognized, accepted and even encouraged" and the pattern remains or a carbon copy of it, at the very least.

However, these widely publicized sexual activities used in films, etc., represent only part of the truth. Fortunately, there are more joyful alternatives like *Outercourse,* which is significantly similar to the concept of *Ecological Love.*

Chapter 5

Freedom

Another part of this reality is more internal, less noticeable, more private and personal in nature. Feelings of well-being are universal and most likely are the ones that drive human beings forward: they are the essence of human nature. However, these feelings are not largely promoted, despite being constantly expressed in the arts. Yet, from a human standpoint, this part of reality is of the greatest importance. The feminist movement has been able to reexamine and reinstate in our bodies, and indeed in our lives, these feelings of well-being which are paramount to our sexual pleasure and can best be described as “sacred energy”.

In light of the emphasis placed on these “feelings” instead of the ones that glorify reproductive patterns and their carbon copies, we discover in homophobic remarks signs of a twisted vision, deeply engrained in the most vicious minds on the planet. In fact, there are evil minds who immediately object to the friendship between same-sex persons, thus demonstrating by their anger that stereotyped and deviated patterns haunt their judgement.

In fact, when two friends hold hands or gently kiss, homophobes immediately suspect, without really knowing what is going on, that these individuals have specific types of sexual activities namely, penetration, sodomy and fellation. However, these practices are a far cry from reality. In their testimonies, many “gay” people say they are uncomfortable with the heterosexual model and its genital aspects. They prefer sensuous relationships and want more affectionate relationships that will also lead them to sexual ecstasy, instead of the genitally-oriented ones. Of course, the more indoctrinated ones engage in sexual activities such as sodomy, but according to my sources, these people come from the heterosexual community – and they do not know any better. They would be more inclined to wallow in unsafe sex activities which in no way correspond to real homophile values and feelings. Same-sex persons are not inclined to play such degrading roles. We love to respect one another and develop healthy and intense relationships based on solidarity, through affectionate feelings.

We also see, among the “gay” population, a strong presence based on friendship and cooperation which characterizes the unbreakable bond formed by “gay” alliances. Respect, love, friendship and harmony are what best define this community’s activities.

Thankfully, in post-war years, we are seeing a decline in diktat strength. As well, less and less people engage in behaviours the industry would like to see them do.

This dearly won freedom has lead us to rethink the education we have received so that when we come together we do so from a spiritual, peaceful and loving place. We freed ourselves from the oppression of imperialist dictatorship which yearned to treat us like pawns on a personal and professional chessboard and as consumers of their goods who have no souls and no value.

In fact, in our modern societies, we see an increase in liberated populations where birth numbers are more natural. This trend towards sustainable development is followed by a more equitable distribution of resources: organic planting is increasing, permaculture is gaining momentum, participatory and democratic cooperation and socially responsible activities are increasingly being adopted. Beauty, goodness, peace and harmony are finally settling in!

But alongside this more natural evolution, dictatorship still tries to lurk its head surreptitiously within the darkest corners of our modern societies in turmoil. In fact, we note the presence of sub-groups operating from a theocracy perspective with its own laws and where forced reproduction is still a centrally-imposed diktat. Forced and compulsory procreation prevails within these tiny groups and is first and foremost in their minds. Everything is based on the fundamental principal that mating is done between “f/m” with the view of establishing a family. Population growth is an obsession, in particular for controlling territories. This phenomenon has spread to many countries, and democratic institutions have remained incredulous in the face of such a conspiracy.

Human settlement is openly used as a weapon in wars of conquest. From a scientific, human and sociological perspective, healthy minds will agree with me that it is totally “unethical” to want to rapidly increase the population among ethnic groups. Who will have more children, that is the real reign of terror and it is completely incompatible with the ideology of liberty which is such a passionate issue for us.

What we are seeing today is a fierce opposition between totalitarianism and freedom, one constantly infiltrating into the other. A country’s borders, which serve to protect the laws and frameworks governing a freedom chosen and promoted by the country, are filled with hordes of expatriates attempting, in the full light of day, to abduct these foreign territories by establishing their own political and social systems, their own theocratic rules as well as their own corresponding civil and criminal codes.

In order to confront the situation, those who defend freedom must implement control mechanisms to safeguard the ethical assets of so-called democratic countries dealing with these problems. Also, there is a growing understanding about this important challenge, when a fierce theocracy tries to assert itself at the very heart of a given society and in doing so, jeopardizes the very principle of freedom for each individual. It’s in the interest of democracy to keep its eyes wide open in the face of what is nothing more than an intellectual shell game which, under the guise of multiculturalism and the right to freedom of religion, make shrewd demands in order to highjack the freedom of political systems and the freedom of civil and criminal codes.

In theocratic systems everything stems from religion, vicious elements want to impose their own political system and dictatorial laws under the guise of multiculturalism and the freedom of religious principle. Except that even in democratic countries, religious freedom (relationships between human beings and heaven), does not equal political freedom (how governments are organized), nor civil code freedom (regulates relations between people), nor criminal code freedom (criminal laws subject to criminal prosecution in a given country). In this way, democracy and its codes apply equally to all citizens, regardless of their beliefs. The law is the law.

In this context, it is totally against humanitarian ethics to force a rapid increase in population. In fact, this logic presupposes that in order to impose any hegemony on values one must enter into a competition of "who will make more children"!!!! That is exactly what free populations are up against at this time. How else is one supposed to view the arithmetic progression of the demographic increase of a population who is forced and obliged to reproduce, and multiply at the dizzying rate of 6 children per couple.

It is easy to understand that such numbers will undoubtedly sound sweet to the ears of dictators, who, in just a few generations, will see a potential increase in profits from the growing number of their subjects and from the forcible taking of highly coveted territories.

Chapter 6

Ethics and Population Growth

Therefore, 6 x 6 x 6 x 6 x 6 x 6 = 46,656, thus, for each original couple, at the 6th generation, it is possible to reproduce 46,656 human beings. According to testimonies, a possible scenario for human beings born in a totalitarian theocracy and determined to defend their religion, would be to quietly but surely take over a certain amount of space where mandatory reproduction stands at its centre, imprisoned in their own system of thought, judging others according to their own codes, laws and visions and where non-members of their communities are despised and banned.

The limitlessness of the numbers is mind-boggling and will certainly appeal to most corrupt governments – who are sometimes suspected of being avid drug users of poisonous or psychotropic substances – who want to frantically enforce their dictatorship by implementing a far-reaching strategy for population growth. This is the description of all sorts of leaders who are obsessed by a maximum increase in population growth and its multiplier effects for generating wealth and who widely approve the rise of great fortunes precisely linked to this phenomenon.

This demeaning regime with its commandments and punishments has victimized a lot of people, particularly in American countries during the post-war period, where church and state were in cahoots with one another. Whoever deviated from this was excommunicated and subject to the worst kinds of threats and abuses. One case was reported where an owner saw her home pillaged and burned by the parish priest and his followers for simply having remained single.

The entire population was forced to copulate within this atrocious authoritarian system. However, in the seventies, the people of Europe and America succeeded in completely dismantling the bodies that forcibly imposed this authoritative power.

Where we had hoped to find the theme of universal love in all kinds of religions, we discovered instead that everyone had given into and accepted a pattern in which reproduction was the main attraction. We are also very familiar with this. Thanks to the Quiet Revolution and feminism, the citizens of Quebec have succeeded in developing a society with a strong sense of freedom, its most basic tenet being free will in the face of the spectre of human reproduction.

Thanks to the strength and fierceness of the people involved in the liberation movement and those advocating humanism, many communities were able to move away from the influence of post-war totalitarianism.

The idea here is not to compare political systems at the expense of one political thought over another, but basically to defend the existence and determination, specifically in our part of the world, of this pure asset called reproductive freedom!

But this freedom must be introduced as is, to new citizens, newborns and newly arrived individuals.

Our greatest power is to be free and to defend this freedom. To be happy and free involves love, respecting ourselves and others, and respecting the political system and the civil and criminal codes of a country.

Chapter 7

Solidarity

In solidarity, the action is accomplished with such grace. The choice of a person to partake in the act of reproduction at any time during her or his life, in a free country, inevitably leads to a more balanced society in relation to the availability of resources. One must have the courage to choose truth and honesty with respect to one's ability to reproduce and to make informed decisions due to the seriousness of this act. Championing freedom of choice demonstrates an extremely important ecological standpoint whose particular role is to reinstate the natural aspect of demography and its environmental impact.

This societal project represents the best of the new millennium, the majority of us having chosen to respond by taking in hand the reins of our own destiny to fight against the current overpopulation in a non-aggressive way.

Democratic laws based on the respect for peace and freedom are very clear, thus every legal means must be deployed to guarantee the continued existence of humanist values within the borders of democratic countries.

As I am sure, enforced reproduction is humanly unacceptable and could be seen as one of the principal causes of serious global social problems such as poverty and violence.

So, in trusting our human intelligence, our human instincts, our consciousness and our thinking power we are inclined to believe that natural human reproduction is a vehicle for success.

But, in order to guarantee access to freedom of choice, we must ensure that the information circulating about human reproduction reflects the right values, and that the teachings transmitted are in harmony with the principle of freedom of association and thus are exempt of any homophobia.

Wonderful work is being done at the moment in order to reinstate the respect that is due to individual choices, friendships, and to eliminate undue pressure when dealing with the freedom to express certain behaviours related to clothing and other details in the way a person looks.

Fortunately, we are witnessing the dismantlement of the systemic rigidity found in numerous households on account of the church, the state and the people themselves, and which had to quickly evolve, because of this hellish system in which every human being had to observe rites and dress codes that were degrading, to say the least.

In order to uphold this unwavering position for reproductive freedom, one must adamantly defend the right to choose what we wear – taking into account the rules of decency of course – our hairstyles, the freedom to choose who we associate with, and with whom we want to express our affection.

Clearly, any teachings contrary to these principles, including acts of terror, violate the laws of democratic societies. We will continue to put forward our convictions contained in our codes and charters to ensure that those guilty of violating fundamental rights are informed of the manner in which they will be judged on their acts, when appropriate, including the teaching of hateful words which is surely the most reprehensible.

In Canada and elsewhere, a national forum should be planned on those sensitive subjects. For example, it is of the utmost importance that the clause issued in paragraph 3, subsection b) be removed from section 319 of the Criminal Code of Canada as it violates the values and undermines Canada's legal position on propaganda and violence – *see chapter 12* –.

What kinds of spaces are reserved for human beings today? What are the other alternatives in a society, when all other possible options, other than the principal choice, imply rejection? In fact, at the present time mating scenarios are still so restrictive that countless individuals do not recognize themselves even in the more common definitions.

Take a label attached to a person like "homosexual". Let's say that in correct English, homogeneity is composed of 2 elements, therefore, a relationship between two people can be described as a homosexual one, but it does not refer to only one individual. So to ask "Are you a homosexual?" is a question where the syntax is completely incorrect. The real question to ask would be: have you had a sexual relationship with a person of the same gender as yourself?

On of the first pitfalls is in identifying another person's gender. How would we otherwise call a relationship between two intersex persons who have not yet defined their own gender identity? Gay or straight? In order to accept the principle of respect towards intersexuality, one must consider 3 genders. Therefore the question of homosexuality or heterosexuality diminishes in importance, as it is sometimes difficult to distinguish between gender and identity. Consequently, we are more inclined to convey the same status to all other possible types of relationships: f/m, f/i, m/i, f/f, m/m, i/i.

Chapter 8

Intimacy

In fact, for the concept of *Ecological Love,* the importance is not in knowing the gender of the people in relationships, but what kind of intimate relationships they have.

How do we define the degree of intimacy in a relationship? The line is not always clear between a friendly relationship and a sensuous one, although some people believe or want us to believe that there is a consensus on this.

How can you best define a sexual relationship? Officially, we most often speak of coitus, its first definition being the penetration of the penis into the vagina. My aim is focused precisely against these prejudicial definitions that grossly integrate abusive customs and categorizations. Is a sexual relationship always a relationship when genitals are touched? Are we talking about the activity or the feeling? Is there room to experience sensual pleasure? Doesn't defining a sexual relationship solely by its reproductive aim, exclude the fact that our libido has its own internal mechanisms that reach far beyond a strictly genital activity?

In fact, we can just have a very exciting and sensual relationship and experience orgasm and all, without touching the genitals identified as being part of the dualistic woman/man relationship.

For instance, what about genital sex, it too can be devoid of pleasure for one or the other or both partners, and can lead to horrific atrocities. Some blogs widely report that more than 40% have confessed they did not really find genital sex pleasurable.

But regardless of the percentage, it is quite clear that common or implicit definitions, general or broader expressions used extensively to describe various ways to penetrate the body, does not do justice to the greatness and beauty of the real or desired experience itself.

There are so many aberrations in this area, especially when it comes to vaginal secretions. It is inconceivable – but nonetheless so real – that some groups consider vaginal secretions to be a sign of uncleanliness...In fact, it happens in South Africa (*Cf. THE LANCET, Volume 352, Page 1292, October 17, 1998. Concerns voiced over "dry sex" practices in South Africa*), where vaginal secretions are quite simply sucked out to dry up the vaginal opening before having sex. And it goes without saying that after that penetration becomes quite painful for the woman!!!! This is one more proof that any feelings of sensuality are prohibited and that sentimentality has no place in the human reproductive act for either partner.

In related approaches, let us mention the unbelievable religious rule which seeks to impose on women the fact that they should not feel pleasure!! The simple fact that it is even thinkable to repress one's own pleasure is an absolute aberration. First of all, every human being knows that intimate and personal pleasure is completely and always present in us – of course at varying levels depending on the time – it can be felt when seeing an elephant, a marine mammal, a man, a woman, an intersex person, or an unanticipated increase in wages, a substantial gain, a business success, the sale of property, the site of a highway or a rainforest, a city and its skyscrapers or a salmon river, eating freshly picked blueberries, strawberries, cherries, raspberries or raw carrots, and so on!

But people belonging to various religious communities are still trying, even today, to go against human pleasure. However, pleasure is everywhere, as is the divine. It's everywhere, and it always has been. We cannot escape it. It is quite impertinent to even think of imposing a view to oppose it. One must be completely outside his or her own body not to feel the sheer joy when we are filled with libido or sacred energy. That is a fact. Libido is personal, it evolves and is felt in different situations and circumstances, and far exceeds the human will. It is a prime source of information on what is happening in our own existence and inspires our creativity. It teaches and inspires us in our work, our business developments, in our art, etc., etc.! Libido is a question of feeling and exists a priori. It is within us, period. Our relationship to the outside world is infinite and so is our relationship to energy and magnetism.

Without further ado, we can probably safely say that the question "have we had a sexual relationship with such and such a person" lacks in precision and elegance...

At certain times, when walking on the street, or alongside a river, or the sea, we think of a person we love and we are filled with a sacred energy. Is it sexual or sensual? The fact of the matter is that something very intimate and personal has happened, and it once again shows that genitality alone is not the queen of pleasure.

Therefore, why not speak of a sexual experience rather than a relationship, because after all, it's the feeling that is important.

Also, who wants to "know" what, exactly, about this sensitive subject? Who is asking the question, to whom and for what purpose? Those are crucial details to know...

What expectations do we have today about relationships? What pictures have we formed in our minds about this?

In this new century, in certain circles, it has become a huge trend in literature to define what is attractive in sexual relationships: a series of practices including cunnilingus, fellation and more recently the cult of anilingus. It has become practically normal among certain human beings who think of themselves or believe themselves to be more modern, to boast about such practices and even transform them into a rigid model that apparently one cannot move away from. And this trend, international in nature, values the practice of anilingus! Wow!

(Cf. *www.terrafemina.com/.../22518-sodomie-**anulingus**-les-derrieres-du-sex...*12 févr. 2013) (in French only)

Oh, please! Should I be surprised! Basic elements of biology inform us of the potential occurrence of dangerous diseases caused by anal secretions... Do we not teach our children scrupulously, at a very young age, how to manage their bodily wastes – at one year old, they all know this... –.

They are taught hygiene practices, how to clean their orifices, how to avoid playing with their excrements precisely because there is a very real threat of transmitting bacterial infections. So how can these young people be asked to believe, or forced to think that sexual relationships will suddenly ignore these wise teachings?

Of course biology and microbiology laws carry an unfortunate inevitability whereby diseases do not instantly appear, but can be delayed. It is therefore difficult to show that there is a causal principle in this situation, how can – sexuality – go to such lengths...The number of young people, adolescents and adults, who fall prey to these sometimes benign or more serious situations is quite appalling.

You must also hear what is being said about it: trivializing or validating however subtly, this type of physical touching like – sodomy, anilingus, etc. – is quite symptomatic.

Seen as mere transgressions and viewed innocently as a source of pleasure, anal sexual practices are more and more widely used. Massages, *anilingus*, sodomy.

***Anilingus** is an oral and anal sex act where one person stimulates the anus of another person by the use of their mouth, including the lips, tongue and/or teeth.*
*(Cf. en.**wikipedia**.org/**wiki**/Anilingus).*

Have a read this correctly…are they really sources of pleasure…Ah, I have no doubt these practices produce sexual responses... Already I can smell this, but ironically, I would say: people must feel really proud to have their anus or perineum sexually stimulated by mouth. But, oh! oh! The consequences are far from being glorious!!

One must make the connection between a practice seemingly harmless, and the subsequent feelings of sickness derived from it. This connection is not always arrived at by the partners or the medical profession. Is the pressure too great? Is the persuasive force of the images one sees in cinemas or on the Internet – spreading tirelessly questionable information about pleasure – to huge?

Producers, screenwriters and directors creating such projects clearly come from a culture that is still generally influenced and degraded by dictatorship.

Forcing sexual reproduction activities tends to make more attractive the frenzied invasion and exploration of the inside of the body by its orifices, and in so doing creates a fantasy where the penetration of various objects is encouraged and its consequences trivialized. In any case, there exists a real frenzy for any type of intrusion when one adopts such an obscure model.

Again, this demonstrates how offensive the fusional nature of this single model is, and how certain persons who are marginalized because of it, find it too invasive.

One easily understands that in the past human reproduction was encouraged to increase an already fragile population or due to the presence of wolves or to counter any other threats. However, under the present circumstances, soaring demography and overpopulation have been reported as serious obstacles to the well-being of the

Earth's population, and humanely speaking, we must stand in solidarity if we wish to reduce our numbers. We must do this by stopping any form of dictatorship which forces people to reproduce. So, it goes without saying that the humanitarian issue is of the utmost importance!

Chapter 9

Conception-Contraception

On the one hand, dictatorships impose forced human reproduction by violence, and on the other, the results of this imposition are totally devastating for numerous countries claiming to be democratic.

The consequences of a reproductively-oriented sexuality are quite distressful. Let us look at all the efforts medicine and official pharmacopoeia have made in order to counteract conception. Where good management of the dynamics involve would suffice to avoid any complication, there is a systematic medicalization of sexuality through the use of a range of objects such as creams, tampons, cervical caps, diaphragms, contraceptives, sometimes used with spermicide in order to improve their effectiveness, etc., etc......All sorts of methods, caps, domes, reusable for years to come – wow! What kind of soap do we use to wash them? Where do we store them? Would we also need a sterilizer? –. It would not be exagerated to say that the range of products available is staggering to say the least.

It is one thing for people to choose to participate in scientific research to develop solutions in order to practice this type of sexuality, but to present it as the only possible choice is untenable.

How do you live if you are one of those people who do not feel comfortable with the official principles of these sexual practices? How do you cope with the fact that your values are not respected and are generally not well represented in the information media sector? Often, people who are looking for pure relationships often find themselves secluded or excluded. And yet, they are most likely to be very sensitive, more conscious of their own pleasure, more inclined to value the happiness of feeling gentleness, truth, simplicity relaxation and delight!

The *Ecological Love* model pays tribute to these people for their authenticity in clarifying the situation and in offering more natural and vibrant solutions to people young and old!

Hence, even informed people agree that these wonderful sexual practices that give rise to feelings of ecstasy and ease surely do not have anything to do with misguided, irritating and uncomfortable sexual activities that cause pain, disillusionment, cancer and other afflictions...

When you are a teenager do your dreams of love and Cupid inevitably fizzle out when you are faced with a large array of suggestions as to what kinds of dangerous and imperfect precautions you have to take! As if sadistic pleasure suddenly took the place of playfulness, a very grim picture befalls these young souls...whereas *Ecological Love* is easy – although it does require an undeniable sense of awareness and vigilance on their part – inspiring, pleasing, soothing and uplifting spiritually, physically, emotionally, sensuously and sexually.

Does your heart hesitate between the two?

The idea in this book is to promote the theory of *Ecological Love* as a viable, pure and simple alternative among other existing models, with its benefits as well as its requirements, depending on the circumstances.

The concept of *Ecological Love* represents a healthy and delightful alternative to health professionals who help patients restore their health and coaches who focus on understanding and improving their clients' performances as well as young and old alike who want to experience sexual pleasure instead of pain.

We all live here on Earth, and if some people want to destroy or debase others.....those who love life, have a very different purpose.

Intelligent people know wisdom and understand clearly human logic where good always prevails. In all our actions, even the smallest ones, this principle takes precedence. And every human being experiences this every day.

Circumstances and times have changed. In 1967, the women's liberation movement gained momentum and in all walks of society gender roles were destigmatized.

A request was submitted which would allow women to become priestesses and celebrate church sacraments. In North American countries, there existed a spirit of cooperation, and in Quebec since the clergy was all in favour of sharing these sacred tasks, they were just about ready to agree to open up their ranks to women. But the Vatican refused in a very offhanded manner, the presence of women in its midst. To undermine the recognition of the undeniable contribution women could bring to the churches' various areas of expertise had a profound impact on those who aspired to key positions, so, eventually, they abandoned institutionalized religious practices to devote themselves to charitable work in an independent context.

The following is a revealing testimony on the subject:

"We wanted to be ordained into the priesthood and everywhere we spoke up the church starting shaking in its boots for fear we were going to invade its pulpits, but that is exactly what we were going to do. Then, an order was given to remove all the pulpits from churches and make them disappear, but I did not know where the ordonnance came from. So, what was said was done...we had so much to say, especially after twenty years of submissiveness orchestrated by church and state, our hearts were very heavy."

Below are comments from another person as well:

"After having given birth to seven children, they grew up, boycotted the church, and when I talked to these young people, I quietly realized they were right to disavow some of the church's positions... I had noted despicable inconsistencies, namely the obligation to conceive to which I had adhered to...I saw that the rules set out were very different whether you were a francophone or an

anglophone...I quickly understood...with all the scandals that were coming to light...that the Vatican had an immeasurable fortune and was suspected of investing in weapons, munitions, birth control pills, etc...It was quite outrageous for me to realize I had been duped because I upheld these beliefs! And that is what I felt also about the increase in poverty as shown on television and in the ever-increasing number of documentaries on the world's poor – while the Vatican, who had amassed billions, stood by and did nothing. If the church told us that we were obliged to procreate, why then did she completely disregard the fate of her children? Even when my daughter told me she wanted to become a priest and was aiming for the papacy, turning her down dashed all her hopes and it felt like a cold shower to her. It would have been quite normal for the Vatican to at least accept her application to become a priest. It became clear to me that we were probably more catholic than the pope...We had integrated values of kindness, of sharing our work, of self-giving and of unconditional love. We loved to love, we knew about health and hygiene rules. So we left, and took with us our wonderful values. We left religion, the church and still today, we continue to move forward with those wonderful values."

In fact, it is not just a question of rejecting the past. Perhaps it might have been necessary for us to multiply like we did in order to advance the world. Let's give ourselves the benefit of the doubt. However, as we speak, and in light of all that is going on in the world, increased tensions, and human hardship reaching intolerable levels, many people are trying to say how they feel about our exponential growth, and that it would be of significant benefit if its pace slowed down in a more efficient and peaceful way.

As well, many products available on the market and used in diverse industries have harmful effects on our health such as certain types of poisons contained in fertilizers and used to grow vegetable crops, for example, or insecticides, or waves emitted by electronic devices that cause numerous fetal deformities: this is hardly a context to give birth, so first, we need to address the serious problems of protecting the quality of the environment in which we want to give birth to our children.

Love between same-sex people is increasingly recognized as

normal. We shout loud and clear that the time has come to make peace with this matter.

Whom we choose to enter into a relationship with is increasingly encouraged by the younger generation. This inevitably leads to freer and less systematic, more diffuse and more sensitive reproductive practices, where we hope all children to come will benefit from adequate support and if need be, will be helped by people who have legitimately chosen not to start a family, but want to offer supportive resources now and then.

Gone are the days when "f/m" had to engage in forced reproduction! Everyone wants freedom, peace and children conceived naturally. This is precisely what is happening in our free societies today, citizens have the advantage of living a healthy love without threats or judgements.

As we have modified religious texts and transformed educational systems during the1980's, 90's and the years 2000, in order to adapt teaching tools and textbooks so they more closely reflect the values surrounding respect and gender equality by introducing new content and gender-neutral teachings, we will also, in the years to come, make very sure that the teachings of doctrines present in writings and audiovisual documents, and implemented by theocratic factions living in democratic territories, are also reformed. Let us mention some of the dogmas that promote exclusion – from scientific and medical fields or public knowledge in general – according to gender and domestic violence: totally unacceptable concepts in democratic countries.

The right to self-determination is precisely at the centre of world disputes. Indeed, everything is unfolding as if this critically important issue is at the very core of current world conflicts. This should raise a flag as to the importance of understanding the whys and the wherefores of this confrontation which would no less greatly benefit, from being conducted in a peaceful manner.

Thankfully, this intense and irreversible global movement to recognize the very foundation and the virtues of the *Ecological Love* concept (IIMEL) ensures that a debate between cultures, on this very touchy issue, can take place in a very peaceful atmosphere!

Part three: *POSITIONING*

Chapter 10

Ecological Love

A love where the true well-being of partners is valued in such a way that it respects their physical and mental health, including humanitarian, ecological and therefore demographic, sociological, economical dimensions, etc., that involves respecting personal and inner feelings, individuality, solitude, free association and shared feelings: that is what *Ecological Love* is all about.

Ecological Love is mindful of human beings and of honest communication where performances revolve around a high level of human concern. For these reasons, it goes against prescribed relationships which unfailingly leave in their wake such horrible devastation as we hear conversations being transmitted on all sorts of weblogs. Not only are the endless complexes of one or the other described, but also the pain of those who have been unjustly classified as being abnormal when their feelings remotely deviate from the established norm.

However much we say that sexuality is a personal issue, the dominant view is very strong and very widespread. It is also a rigid system which quickly evaluates what is normal.

It is not uncommon to read stories of partners who are quite uncomfortable, with having oral sex. Actually, it would seem that nearly 50% of people do not appreciate this as it is often perceived by them as being a degrading and demeaning practice.

According to recurring reports, sexologists advise their clients to comply with such activities, and they are also told that it is a proof of love when they take a penis into their mouth, as it demonstrates esteem and can be an immensely rewarding message... Also, these same specialists may denigrate, depending on the circumstances, those who in no way recognize themselves in this.

What blatant antagonism! What appears to be demeaning for some would allegedly be very rewarding for others...Quite a major difference of opinion that should be cleared up between the partners right from the start, agreed!!

Mainstream rhetoric blithely promotes this type of intrusion even if it is contrary to the will of large sections of the population, so it would be a good idea to assess how widespread the practice is.

One only needs to see how this trend vehemently defends penetration as being the only natural sexual practice, even in democratic societies. It is also quite astonishing to see how this is strangely akin to teachings carried out in several countries where it is clearly said that: “only reproductive sex is natural, non reproductive sex is non natural”. This is indeed an arrogant assertion on the part of democratic countries whose charters are supposed to recognize the principles of freedom, protection and well-being of a person and claim that all human beings have equal value and dignity.

In a more insidious way, the modern version of the concept says that “making love” is strictly a sexual act with the intention of reproducing (whether or not there is contraception and its acceptance).

With this aim in mind, it is quite unimaginable to think of having pleasurable moments without referring to reproduction. Even though there have been changes since 1975, we note that the young people of today are still continuously being subjected to the “conception”/ “contraception” principle.

In order to counteract this situation, it is absolutely necessary to create an alternative that truly represents the values of freedom and empowerment that must be made available to everyone.

As well, in some circles it is quite acceptable to adopt the “hard” model in which all fantasies seem to be allowed. The rule of brutal sexual genitality – which often ignores human biology – is in full swing with its numerous sexual objects, of which some are quite problematic to say the least. They cause infections, and the list is growing as new products are being introduced into the market, and yes, introduced as well into the body of one another with such flippancy, and maintained as such, by the medical profession who strives to find drugs whose side effects, sometimes clearly labelled, are just as harmful as the disease they are supposed to heal.

For example, we've seen drugs used for erectile dysfunction claiming to have secondary effects, including facial redness, headaches, etc. Whoops!! What a contradiction, to want to solve an erection problem while at the same time embarrassing the subject by saying he might have facial redness. This might inevitably lead to a decrease in self-esteem and libido. Or those unhappy patients who suffer from premature ejaculation and are quickly advised to take the appropriate steps to get psychological help in order to heal from their pseudo-trauma, and maybe take a little prescribed drug...well, well....

As we know, penetration is not the answer for everyone, so is it not more normal to respect the fact that each person should live according to his or her own feelings of pleasure?

And moreover, in other cases, should a decrease in libido be viewed as a fault sometimes, rather than just a reality to shoulder that can be dealt with according to one's own desire.

It goes without saying that partners do not always feel the same things at the same time, and often the best response to adjusting the sacred energy between lovers is to keep it simple and even to transcend it.

In the 21st century, a great number of sexual diseases are created in the world. Public health services are quite shaken by the alarming increase in the incidence of infections.

Has institutional psychology promoted dangerous sexual practices and pretended they were necessary in order to feel pleasure? What principles underline this twisted viewpoint?

Consider the conception/contraception belief system. No other area of a person's life or of a business corresponds to this demoralizing logic. How can one possibly imagine a person sowing seeds in the earth then watering them with a poison preventing germination? No one does of course. Then, why would so few dispute the conception/contraception logic? Especially since this concept challenges the very foundations of modern sexology, yes?

Chapter 11

Natural Reproduction

Natural reproduction is the key to success and comes with personal and social responsibilities. But in order for reproduction to effectively be "natural" one should nevertheless recognize the right to a non reproductive sexuality and not one modelled after it. In some religions this is inconceivable, but in democratic society, it is essential.

To experience a natural, simple, healthy and sacred sexuality with the utmost respect is a change in the progress made since the last century, especially in large urban centers like Montreal or elsewhere in America, in Europe and around the world, wherever we promote the freedom to be one's self!

It is a purely joyful and simple way to live where reflection and communication about ecological reproduction are steeped in wisdom and easily experienced. And if some feel discomfort in this, others are at ease with it.

In pursuit of more modern sexual practices, some people are well adjusted to the dominant model while others experience great discomfort. However, and I am sure you will agree, for those who suffer from this situation, it is time to raise a white flag and demand we put a stop to systemic discrimination against a healthy sexuality that is sometimes considered childish or not up to the level of a more genitally-oriented and high risk sexuality, in which it appears that one is literally pushed to enter, very often without his or her knowledge – from adolescence onwards.

These days, there is no doubt that ecology is at the forefront. In all areas we are trying to reposition ourselves in order to make better choices regarding our commitments. The meaning of our actions continues to evolve. In all scientific fields and their applications as well as in everyday life, we endeavour to behave responsibly, more intelligently, more humanly and more naturally.

To address *Love* in such a way appeared to me to be quite commendable!! We must clearly identify the motives behind each of our activities and the ecological impact it has on us, our environment and our development.

Healthy *Love* has without a doubt existed since the dawn of time. The blissful moments which transport us...The wonderful closeness and poetry in our sweet glances...The lingering touches and joyful feelings of love...oh! Yet, these warm connections are considered to be unnatural in lands under dictatorship rule.

It's mind-blowing how this seemingly endless gap divides the population worldwide!

And taken all together, it's incredible to see how numerous aspects of peace-building have swept through our lands in the form of valued initiatives which propose that we all live life according to our convictions and despite our differences.

If human beings really want to define separate areas in which to pursue their diametrically opposed visions, this is precisely why we have borders: to circumscribe national experiences. Each country has its codes, and those who recognize that every human being has rights and freedoms, that respect and dignity are the foundations of justice and peace, are called upon today to promote their beliefs and hold an urgent debate around human relationship values which includes *Love* and sensuality. Effectively, the purpose of *Ecological Love* is to bring together views about the real facts and indisputable truths, position itself advantageously as a viable alternative and interpret dynamically the thinking of numerous others.

Chapter 12

Incitement to Violence and Hate Propaganda

Current provisions in Article 319 of the Canadian Criminal Code appear to be inconsistent, only religious texts seem to have special status giving them the right to spread hate propaganda. On the Government of Canada website, one can read the following:

"Hate propaganda: Any writing, sign or visible representation that advocates or promotes genocide or the communication of which by any person would constitute an offence under section 319."

Section 319, subsection (1) states:

"Every one who, by communicating statements in any public place, incites hatred against any identifiable group where such incitement is likely to lead to a breach of the peace is guilty of

(a) an indictable offence and is liable to imprisonment for a term not exceeding two years; or

(b) an offence punishable on summary conviction."

Section 319, subsection (2) also states:

- *"Everyone who, by communicating statements, other than in private conversation, wilfully promotes hatred against any identifiable group is guilty of:*
- *(a) an indictable offence and is liable to imprisonment for a term not exceeding two years;*
- *(b) an offence punishable on summary conviction."*

However, it is quite disturbing to read in Section 319, subsection 3 of the Canadian Criminal Code the following:

"*No person shall be convicted of an offence under subsection (2) in the following circumstances:*

Subsection (b), if, in good faith, the person expressed an opinion on a religious subject based on a belief in a religious text...." *(Cf.* http://laws.justice.gc.ca/feng/lois/C-46/page-159.html)

It is absolutely inconceivable that religious texts produce documents inciting to violence without recrimination, thus unjustly benefitting from a democratic government whose criminal code allows written or oral communications the right to promote hatred.

Instead, we would have expected religious people to advocate decency and love, so it was quite a surprise for us to find out they would want to make hateful statements and be acquitted for this at the same time. Now is the time for Canadian government lawyers to amend this legislation urgently, under the present circumstances, as it goes against all humanistic values.

Let us be inspired by the respectful words of *Arthur Rimbaud, March 1870*, as translated by Oliver Bernard: *Arthur Rimbaud, Collected Poems (1962) in a few verses of his poem:*

Sensation

On the blue summer evenings

I shall go down the paths,

Getting pricked by the corn

Crushing the short grass:

In a dream I shall feel

It's coolness on my feet.

I shall let the wind

Bathe my bare head.

.....But endless love

Will mount in my soul...

It is *Charlebois* (Robert Charlebois, Quebec singer-songwriter) as an adult, who later on, put to music those infinitely tender words...

One of the world's most important issues are threats designed to subjugate entire populations to authoritarian regimes where sexual behaviours are based on mandatory reproduction. This hostile domination is imposed, in certain cases, by weapons and reinforced on a larger scale through education, cinematography, literature, music, theatre, etc.

Behaviours officially recognized as being acceptable, are those seemingly leading to the proliferation of human beings and governed by completely different interests than the well-being of individuals.

It's surprising to note the ease with which certain people like to say that these things are logical and natural activities, and they do it so well, while at the same time giving the impression there is a general consensus around them. The same as with the social representation usually associated with "making love" as being an eternal truth which applies to everyone.

In fact, the portrayal of sexuality has been very much interfered with adulterated, kicked around, falsified, manipulated and fiddled with – and anything else you might want to add – that loving partners would do things to each other that neither of them really appreciates.

Let's take the example of two women, who lived together for thirty-three years, and decided not to practice cunnilingus once they had confided in each other that they had no desire for it. They said it took a certain amount of time and courage to mutually admit they did not appreciate this practice, and how great it was to find out the other partner felt the same, especially given the fact that there is an apparent consensus around sexuality that promotes such practices.

As well, two men living together for twenty-five years confided they had never practiced anal sex. This mutual respect is much more common that we think!!

Other comments heard were from people who did not believe what society considers as a normal sexuality, and complained that their views were seldom accepted.

It is not uncommon to hear of situations where people have been urged to take part in a form of genital sexuality, and if they refuse, they are categorized as having a sexual pathology stemming from their fears, or the rubbles of their past, or other traumas modern psychiatry loves to diagnose, and for which it administers treatment in the form of medication, electroshocks, laser rays or partial or total removal of the cervix.... Nothing is obvious. It's always a gamble.

Many people have told childhood stories when they had an intense but strictly chaste friendship with a same-sex child and were severely condemned by others or even repressed their own selves for doing it.

And how many people who are friends stop seeing one another at the prescribed age or the procreation age because they are of the same sex? So, you meet a person of the opposite sex with whom, even in the worse case, you don't have much in common with, and choose, like many others, to enter into a relationship, even though there is violence and belittling, because it is a heterosexual relationship, and thus corresponds to the only strongly encouraged and prescribed model that exists.

Incitement to violence and hate propaganda in numerous religious texts have to do precisely with intimate relationships between people, whereby a reign of terror has been instituted where the faithful must adopt a pattern of behaviour suggesting the use of violence between them, within a mating scenario exclusively f/m, and where human reproduction is the systematic outcome.

Chapter 13

The Reproductive Model

We surely agree that persons of the female or male gender will have, in all likelihood, nearly one in two chance of having same-sex friends. But what are the chances they will enrich this harmonious understanding or decide to end the relationship in order to conform to the reproductive couple model?

There are so many choices to make: we can live together or not, give birth or not, support one or several children, adopt them or make them ourselves and discuss compensation for the person who will be pregnant for 9 months and have to live with the many consequences associated with it. Leave each with a baby, raise it, send it to work abroad, depending on the country, or a little later send it to work in a factory that benefits the owners rather than the employees, who are often overexploited or living in harsh conditions, or in cooperatives or they go to school and become academics who work for multinationals who become richer at their expense. So this is called loving your offsprings, is it? Or else, in the best case scenario, we are lead to believe we can bequeath a house with a garden to our children when they turn 18 years old, a house owned by their ancestors since the 800th previous generation, and hey, why not, one million years ago!...Let's see traces of the past, why not!

Today, however, many eighteen year olds do not, and I mean literally, do not receive any tangible heritage. Having to start from scratch as if it was the beginning of the world! Others find it quite normal under pretense that there are a lot of opportunities out there of course; but we must be aware that we are competing with other young people who, thanks to their parents, have access to companies, or have opportunities to start one, or own land, horses, yatchs, houses, gardens, etc., etc. They own a car, a laboratory or have connections with people in leading research centres around the world, or in television networks, radio, politics, business, industry or others. This is a huge issue, so it is quite possible your child or other children may be a bit loss when having to face such a situation.

What can one do in a world where they have no place? In a world where an appalling number of people cannot house, feed and clothe themselves or fulfill their dreams? And in countless number of cases, pitfalls do occur, whether or not you are university graduates! You are cast aside...And there is no guarantee that even if your children finish their education they will have the prospect of a decent life.

To be honest about this situation can only be beneficial.

Of course, everywhere there are people who have succeeded in carving themselves a place in the world. So be it. Good for them. However, the problem is not there, it is among those who, a good part of the time, live in hell, in the shadows and in hardship. Presently, in the world – and the following research does not seem to take into account the low levels of accessibility to healthy foods, for individuals in western populations –:

"The Food and Agricultural Organization's (FAO) most recent estimates indicate that 12 percent of the global population...is undernourished...

(cf. http://www.fao.org/docrep/018/i3434e/i3434e01.pdf.)

It is quite common to see unfortunate souls sadly searching for their own path, who want to participate in production activities without ever being able to make it a reality. They have an indomitable spirit, and no way to channel it. They have tremendous potential and are unable to take part in the experimental work chain. They are being sidelined. How many billions are sidelined? According to current statistics, how many billions of people are excluded or neglected? Did the children's parents really know what future they had in store for their offsprings? Is this the gift of life? Thanks, but no thanks! How many testimonies reveal the horrors that are intended for them? Do the people who give life take responsibility for their actions?

During our interviews in Africa, particularly in 1975, many people told us they were *forced* to have children under threats. It's quite impressive to realize there are still people who are responsible for this frantic race towards reproduction while completely ignoring that the living conditions in which these children are born into, are totally inadequate. When will we confront the people responsible for such a manipulation? Do we agree that the earth should be populated in such a horrible way, even against the wishes of the concerned creators of life? It seems that this sort of thing should be brought before the International Tribunal.

Of course the rich can enjoy their good fortune in broad daylight, but the poor, the banished and the neglected people could decide to rebel against their fate. This would create quite a storm and seriously undermine the flow of events, thereby jeopardizing other people's lives. But isn't this exactly what is happening with all the revolts, the lootings, etc.?

The status quo is not a viable alternative. And that is precisely what the *Ecological Love* theory is trying to do: break the deadlock.

It is logical, simple and ecological, we have enough media resources to reach an understanding about personal benefits, social community and how to free ourselves from the weight of the stereotypical mating behaviour.

It is simple and not easy at the same time, to put a stop to the current dictatorship on forced reproduction and to promote the concept that everyone should have access to *Ecological Love*, in order to support more natural demographics based on the respect given to human beings and those yet to come, and the resources currently available.

The fact that everyone has the right to choose is fundamental in a democracy, whereas in a theocracy, only god makes decisions. And it is precisely at a time when making decisions about our intimate life that everything is being played out across the planet.

In many countries, population increases under authoritarian control and creates imbalances on earth, especially at the human level, because often the right to liberty and security is violated and it negatively impacts on our degree of happiness, self-actualization and love – provided these values are considered fundamental of course – at the social level, with respect to the limited access to healthy natural resources, amongst others. A large percentage of newborns will be impoverished and deprived of the essential elements of their health. As well, the abundance of workers it will create will only benefit a low percentage of leaders.

Fortunately, there are improvements coming from more and more people who are socially and responsibly committed to taking back their decision-making power at the social and personal levels in their lives. This phenomenon is growing at such a rate that it exceeds that of a neutrino!

At the same time we are witnessing the emergence of grassroots initiatives and numerous participative actions with great results, both in material terms with environmentally friendly features in cities, towns and countrysides as well as at the economic and human level with an ideally discretionary demography.

Chapter 14

Freedom

In the 70's, the international feminist movement strongly emphasized that rape was a crime when sexual activity was not consensual or took place under threat. To submit under command, violates the freedom of consent principle. Having to submit under constraint of penalties, as it is required in certain societies, is in direct conflict with democratic principles. In the third quarter of the last century women, men and intersex people were given the opportunity to jointly condemn any infringement on their integrity and to refuse categorically any form of submission, especially when it concerned sexual relationships and reproduction.

Witnesses and often collaborators of major achievements and substantial gains at the human rights level in democratic countries, women, men and intersex persons living in theocratic countries – who often found themselves in very precarious situations, even dangerous ones, like spousal violence, and which in no way corresponded to the aspirations of either gender – have specifically asked for help from human rights activists, in the 70's, in the hope that pacifist humanist principles could be respected as well in their own countries. Following these requests, solidarity efforts were undertaken around the world in order to recognize their fundamental rights. A solid global link was thus created between countries.

However, in 1979, an important event took place, and everything changed: a tyrant, upon coming to power, committed a serious political offense in a previously free country. Several groups organized a protest against his despotic demands. During a major demonstration (20,000 people) when the necessity for women to wear veils came into effect in this suddenly theocratic country, several participants were violently assaulted by barbaric attacks, with vitriol, during an event clearly authorized by the government. Buses were filled with poorly dressed people armed with bottles of sulphuric acid, visibly paid, and under the command of a leader, to execute the evil plot of the new dictator...

An international feminist movement American icon, who had been invited to participate in the demonstration – which was taking place in an ultramodern city – inescapably witnessed these devastating scenes. After having been placed in custody herself for a few days, and thinking she would die, she was released against all hopes.

Following her release, and deeply distressed by the cruel nature of these events, she was courageous enough to communicate to the humanitarian community what had taken place. During a conference at McGill University in Montreal, while she was giving an emotional account of what happened during the event, to the 400 participants gathered in an impromptu fashion in the large auditorium and who suddenly became quite frightened when six typical bearded elements – even though the meeting had not been publicized much – stood up abruptly and started yelling at the crowd in a foreign tongue, and chanting loudly vicious words with an arm raised in the air. The crowd, suddenly panicked and tried to get away, but everything cleared up when people started exiting through large open doors.

We realized Montreal had arrived at a turning point and at a certain level, that it was controlled by acts of terrorism. We were being pursued, and it became quite clear we could not express ourselves in a safe environment.

There is no question that the cruelty of the acid attacks is a blatant lack of ethics, and that the pacifist women's movement found itself in a humanitarian deadlock. The deception in the face of this unprecedented violence could be felt the world over, and as a result, many of us decided to put an end to our public demonstrations.

We were more than willing, through our sociological, political and judicial analyses and activities, to contribute to the improvement of life on earth, but definitely not in such a horrific atmosphere. Absolutely not. Our intelligence and peaceful attitude do not tolerate such vile attacks.

This resulted in the cessation or the slowing down altogether of international aid activities in democratic countries on the part of feminist intellectuals. The number of requests from women, men and intersex persons living in theocratic countries to help them fight against their totalitarian governments – who continually subject them to savage attacks from their troops – dwindled down.

It is with deep regret that we chose to leave the public arena and hide, sometimes in makeshift camps, terrorized by the magnitude of the horrors we experienced and the threats we received. Never, to this day, in a democracy, did we ever have to deal with such disrespectful behavior during demonstrations. Never.

On the contrary, as our demands always came from a humanist perspective, the general population and the human rights advocates rapidly gave their unwavering support to a movement, who was, up until then, a peaceful movement. The values of freedom and respect developed over time.

However, some thirty-five years later, the horror has grown as we observe totalitarian theocracies gradually claim more and more space the world over.

As a result, several democratic countries find that misogynistic and misandrous diktats, aided by multiculturalism policies, have been able to break their laws. This is done with the somewhat childish consent of a leftist faction obviously not conscious of the impact such misanthropic behaviours have on entire populations. In fact, this dictatorial situation deprives citizens of all genders, when sexual behaviours become compulsory and where in the spirit of international agreements, it does not respect current freedoms and laws.

It is therefore with great courage that we reiterate our main demands: 1. Respecting a person's integrity; 2. Respecting the principle of equality between women, men and intersex persons;
3. Refusing any attempts to submit girls, women, men and intersex persons to sexual practices which ignore the concept of informed consent (criminalizing rape); 4. Criminalizing forced reproduction;
5. Examining all teachings being done in democratic countries through texts, documents, and audiovisuals so that they are in line with the democratic principles adopted in current civil and criminal codes.

If there is a will on the part of populations living in those democratic countries – and other interested populations – to liberate themselves from theocratic systems that demand their complete submission, and that this common will is shared and has sufficient strength, there will be a happy ending.

We can only have hope that everyone will ally themselves to respect a free world. We would not want to leave newborns and future generations with a legacy of violence within the citizenry.

Experiencing the freedom to manage our own intimate life leads to a more pacifist society where relationships between people will be managed in a much more civilized way. This is exactly what is happening in Quebec and Canada since the development of the humanist movement in the 70's; a civilized and respectful world, where we can live free loving relationships without having to marry or to reproduce...Although this was the case in the 50's.

For the past forty years, we have had less stressful relationships between genders. Comments from other continents are very positive concerning the evolution of Quebeckers, Canadians, Americans and Europeans, just to name a few...

However, sometimes people raised in countries where spousal violence is taught and is compulsory, pacifist attitudes adopted are perceived as being too nice... Here is someone's testimony to that effect:

"We are so gentle with one another, one guy told me... "people are laughing at us...guys from other cultures tell us we are not macho enough, not tough enough with the women here..."This is getting to be quite tedious..."

No doubt when people are hunted down, imprisoned, tortured or killed, because of having ***non compliant intimate relationships*** – tenderness, intercourse or no intercourse, no penetration, no ejaculation, one baby, two babies, not enough babies or no baby at all – then indoctrinated in participating innocently in spousal abuse,...that this can create very strong and indeed intolerable social tensions.

One can clearly see here how important differences in the management of intimate relationships are, and that social tensions will regrettably increase when there is an aggressive sexism component to it, but will greatly diminish when a society has the freedom to explore its libido – simply and intelligently – in a responsible and ecological way.

Chapter 15

Misery

Let's take as an example, a family with seven children where the first three children make the next four feel as if they should not have been born, so that their parents have more time and more money to spend on them. As well, property distribution would have been much more advantageous to them. The same thousand dollars divided by seven or by three does not have the same value for one or for the other. Doesn't the distribution of wealth depends solely on the number of beneficiaries?

Even though many people believe it's possible for anyone to live in harmony and abundance, there is, in fact, half or perhaps two-thirds of the world population living in poverty and suffering.

However, there is every reason to believe that the simple fact of saying to ourselves "yes, we can", is enough to fight off poverty. But we must be free to act creatively if we want to achieve this.

Misery, poverty, extreme poverty, hunger, cold, and handicaps, illnesses and everything they entail, are at the heart of the humanitarian problems of the 21st century. An adequate solution would be to intervene and identify – even criminalize – acts of coercion carried out by any group or sect whose aim is to compel their members or followers to practice "forced reproduction".

Indeed, a dictatorial, authoritarian and terrorist practice whose aim is to indoctrinate others into a belief system in which it is mandatory to copulate, goes against the elimination of poverty and injustice in the world.

It is a daunting task to try and eliminate poverty, and numerous bodies, coalitions, governments, institutions and national and international associations find themselves faced with finding solutions to this terrible human disaster invading our planet, when in other instances, life has the potential to be so great. Does one depend on the other? Is wealth, for some, born out of the enslavement of others? It is important to do something about this.

In order to participate more effectively, and resolve more quickly world problems, taking into account the correlation between demographics and poverty, let us give each other the right to talk about our most intimate human relationships and their social and environmental impact, to finally triumph from an age where we felt silenced, quashed, censured, muzzled, oppressed or reduced for the past thirty-five years and more.

Perhaps this is the first hurdle we must overcome, to express ourselves publicly about all kinds of discomforts and embarrassments and which – under threats of violence – keep us locked into silence.

Knowledge of human biology, whether ancient or modern, is an important indicator as to the impact of our behaviours on the human body and its characteristics.

The right to personal freedom is crucial – and is well entrenched into our Charters of Rights and Freedoms –. This is true. However, it is important to realize that the diktat is quite damaging when it creeps all the way into our intimate relationships.

Let's take, for example, youth meetings – participants are not properly informed and are sometimes placed in an unfortunate situation –, some even find themselves facing a behavioural dilemma between their desire and their determination. How many times are we surprised by the lack of clarity about love experiences, even if the intentions are pure, and when partners choose very loosely, without any preliminaries, and without thinking about how to follow an impulse which should be managed and understood in its essence, "before" participating in any activities, rather than "after".

An adequate exchange on the subject should take place before...and not after. What are the real opportunities available to young people in terms of relationships today?

How is it that in our modern societies today, even the slightest intimate relationship will inevitably lead one to the most obscure shelves carrying synthetic pharmaceutical products? Birth control pills, – that never promised to be completely effective, and have to be taken at the same time, every day, etc... – foams, latex condoms, and any other medication for sale, created precisely for the occasion, all too often have devastating first and secondary effects.

Is the current situation well summarized in La Fontaine's poem: "*They died not all, but all were sick." (Cf.,* ***The Animals Sick of the Plague,*** ***Jean de LA FONTAINE*** *(1621-1695)) (Translated from the French by Elizur Wright)*

How does one justify that natural sexual relationships lead to surgical procedures with profound impacts, such as hysterectomies or vasectomies.

However, let me be precise: far be it for me to condemn the courage of a lover who wants to choose infertility. Without a doubt this effort is perfectly commendable.

Furthermore, in light of current considerations, and knowing that these medical procedures can cause a number of problems, *Ecological Love* proposes a way to avoid such delicate surgeries.

Let us shout in the face of such stupidity – as it plays such a crucial role in the survival of the human race, our lives and our enjoyment of it –, as it is such a disgrace, to prevent citizens from living love freely in a healthy and ecological way.

Let us take a very simple example like experiencing harmless activities in our daily lives with someone of the same gender. It is quite astounding that this kind of friendship can create such controversy, destruction and unspeakable violence.

This flawed logic certainly brings to mind the following question: is the simple fact of wanting to be close to an intersex person an automatic sign of perversity because this person intrinsically carries the same gender as you?

Despicable laws concerning human friendship and human affection, which is hardly an insignificant phenomenon, caught my attention. The disproportionately high negative reaction on the friendship between same-sex persons seems to me to be completely unjustified. The illogical character of such strong opposition has motivated me to continue my research on the subject, in order to unravel the intrigue, for the benefit of society.

I first examined the quality of different types of relationships between people, to rapidly note, among other things, that the same candour exists between same-sex persons and different-sex persons.

Even though choosing our destiny is a fundamental right in democratic countries, on the contrary, in certain countries, under a dictatorship, special measures, even drastic ones, are put in place to fight against friendship between same-sex persons, outlaw celibacy or simply punish someone who does not want to mate or reproduce. And this key issue seemingly played out at the intimate reproductive level, embodies the significant differences between global political systems, and hence, becomes the main source of antagonism in the world.

Chapter 16

Homophobia

It becomes quite clear when analyzing disparities between the values of different countries, that homophobia primarily comes from a desire to use procreation for mercantile purposes. In fact, it is the only plausible explanation when a society has such a difficult time tolerating the fact that people refuse to endorse a model such as the "reproductive couple".

Our study highlights the fact that governments, industrialists and others are able to anticipate and profit from forced human reproduction. As well, would they carry out their indoctrination program through education and brutal repression to establish their standards at a level they find convenient, in order to fulfill their greedy goals?

Do populations really have the same interest in reproducing under pressure? In olden days, it was probably necessary, but today, when faced with such human misery and poor living conditions, it appears that in-depth discussions must take place in order to avoid perpetuating a situation that has already gone far beyond the limits of human understanding.

Actually, if one lived in an atmosphere of complete freedom of association, human reproduction would be quite different. There would be far fewer conception-contraception relationships. The taking of cancerous birth control pills would probably become unnecessary due to an efficient and responsible management of fertility and impregnation processes versus the sensuality and well-being of each individual.

Sexuality would have two distinct features instead of only one. One would be oriented towards reproduction and the other towards gentleness and intimacy, where sperm would take another path rather than with a fatalistic view foisted on entire populations that are held hostages.

While many others adhere to a way of life more closely related to the "reproductive couple" model – whether or not it is dictated by the state, and where everything points to the fact that it is not always a way of life adopted by everyone if they had been totally free to choose – many others do not buy into it, but bear witness to the fact that they have endured terrific pressures, oppressions, total rejection and other forms of discrimination simply because they have chosen to be in much more natural relationships.

Why is it mandatory for sperm to be directed towards the ova when it is quite capable of being released into the environment?!!

Countless people speak quite serenely of their unique friendships with same-sex people as being a natural, simple, ordinary and entirely irreproachable reality. There is absolutely no valid argument that can contradict this affirmation.

Chapter 17

Fallible Practices

What would justify sexual practices that mimic reproductive practices, whereby lovers behave negligently with regard to basic rules of hygiene?

It seemed ludicrous, that males, females and intersex persons would be inclined to practice sodomy and other unsafe practices contrary to any sound knowledge of human biology; the relationship between sexual disease incidences, alarming to say the least, and the popularity of such practices is obvious.

According to our humble opinion, how does one even think of visiting the anus during a loving relationship, when the present moment requires that it should be avoided at all costs? Numerous comments describe the intense pain felt in the behind after such practices, and thus reveal the revolting apathy surrounding this taboo subject.

All our research led us to potential responses to our legitimate questions concerning these errant practices: the model is so firmly rooted in our consciousness due to persistent indoctrination that partners want to imitate reproductive practices, that is, penetration at all costs, despite the potential threat posed by anal secretions and its associated diseases.

Is penetration so indispensable that we can sometimes casually prefer an inappropriate orifice, to say the least? At any rate, it seems that sodomy, for both genders combined, is a very widespread practice around the globe. This practice is also responsible for the incidence of serious sexual diseases that partners do to each other, simply when they visit specific infectious areas of the body. We also know these infections occur when people cannot manage correctly the activities surrounding their own orifices that are more at risk, like precisely the anus...

Chapter 18

Inner Health

We all agree that human fertilization is a very special moment. It is an activity highly directed by our spirit and deserves all our respect and attention. So be it.

We also know, for the benefit of female and male genitors – and of their offsprings – that human fertilization requires a certain amount of basic knowledge acquired in advance, and available in various ways, during each era, in all corners of the Earth.

In fact, since the beginning of time, we have amassed a great deal of knowledge on health, particularly regarding basic hygiene rules about our own orifices.

Because of the physical structure of genders we know how important it is to take specific precautions, especially when it comes to the female of our species. Very little information is available on this subject, so in order to break the silence surrounding this issue, we would like to reveal critical, delicate and intimate information about it.

Speaking of body orifices, we have the ears, the eyes, the nose, the mouth and... others. We know we have to be cautious when we introduce an object into the human body.

Furthermore, the urethra is vulnerable to germs, viruses and others, and can be in contact with mucous membranes or anal fluids, in unsanitary conditions. I agree it is very subtle. However, precious biological data is too often completely ignored or escapes our consciousness, so I hope you will forgive me if I cannot bring myself to not mention it.

Consider the amount of images showing intimate relationships where the movie industry and other media – including Internet – are often the only sources of information available to young people today... The information depicts, describes and documents different types of relationships – as if it corresponds to normalcy –, where there is a real risk of doing serious harm to human health, when depositing even minute quantities of infectious fluids, including anal secretions, into female, male or intersex persons' orifices.

What about when the penis orifice comes into contact with the anus during sodomy, and completely ignores or overlooks the subtle dangers contained in those secretions deposited into the vaginal orifice?

Official literature tells us very little about the vulnerability of internal organs to the fecal waste that can potentially or naturally be sucked into body conduits towards the prostate, the uterus or the ovaries.

What are the damages inflicted to the human body?!! Everything is processed microscopically, but.... it is still processed. Where do we find information on this subject? Where is it? Is it hard to find...

While it is vital for children at a very young age to understand the concept of controlling their urine and bowel movements; all children of course, girls, boys and intersex persons.

Because everyone's body openings are configured differently, some people are not subjected to the same risks with their bodies. First of all, it is important they be informed of the physical implications and health risks linked to the management of their secretions, but they should also understand the subtle differences according to gender. The urethra and anus are set much farther apart in the male than in the female.

Children must learn to take the necessary precautions so as not to infect themselves while cleaning their private parts, for example, after a bowel movement or other, and when in contact with the mouth, eyes, nose, ears, or skin as well. They must also be made aware that the distance between the urethra and the anus is much closer in the "female" body and that the vaginal canal – or, if you please, the sacred orifice – is right in the middle of these two orifices. This increases the potential danger of certain practices, particularly when we know that our organs, even the ones located deeper in the body, are vulnerable to germs and viruses.

Wisdom tells us to abide by the following rule: avoid introducing into our many visible or more intimate orifices any object capable of causing injury, infections, irritations and further suffering that might lead to benign or malignant cancers in human body systems.

The real causes of cancers are still not well documented. However, introducing different substances into body orifices, the urethra – of both men and women and into women's vaginas as well – is suspicious to say the least.

Part Four: *IMPLICATION*

Chapter 19

Offsprings

As the new century begins, we see more and more children stepping up to the barricades as they learn the troubling facts surrounding the stories of their birth. They want immediate explanations and criticize the lack of vision of their creators whom they hold accountable for their carelessness, neglect and irresponsibility, in terms of the health and safety of their offsprings.

What a social blunder to show sexual play in such a cavalier way, as being a series of gestures seemingly unimportant, but with the potential to transform itself, without warning, into a grandiose dramatic presentation resulting in a too often unwanted and unprepared pregnancy.

This happens to people who do not take birth control products, as well as those who told us how ineffective contraceptive pills were. In fact, there are gray areas when taking contraceptive pills and young people find this somewhat hard to accept.

A surprise pregnancy is a bitter pill to swallow for parents as well as for children...but then, you do have to live with it!

Luckily, with the vast knowledge we have acquired up until now about sexual pleasure, we can demonstrate the workings of a healthy, invigorating and enlightened sexuality without interfering with copulation, of course!

When the time comes, young people have a great deal to say about the questionable fate that is in store for them. In fact, what choice do they really have today in a context where procreation appears to be non-negotiable? They are too often faced with only two choices. First of all, females must wear IUDs or take carcinogenic birth control pills while males wear condoms – neither is 100 %

guaranteed, we know this and we ignore this – in order to counter the obsessive interest in conception.

Secondly, women who are uncomfortable with wearing an IUD or taking the pill, and those who are also uncomfortable with surgery, do not have any other choice but to accept their roles as mothers or as fathers.

But in showing only these two choices have we established a truly comprehensive list of other possibilities? No, not by a long shot.

In fact, our research demonstrates that what is missing is the alternative concept of *Ecological Love* which outlines the thoughtful measures on how to live a healthy relationship – without repeated insemination (natural, of course) –. According to the theory of *Ecological Love*, Love itself becomes a truly unique experience instead of a pitfall.

Pure and simple *Ecological Love* calls for a positive sexuality free from pain, denial, sacrifice, risk, control and degradation. Fortunately we live in an age where all this is possible.

In addition to presenting numerous possibilities in order to avoid any confusion in relationships, the theory of *Ecological Love* presents great incentives to practice truly natural, organic, free and ecological procreation.

Ecological Love is a healthy, pure and simple way to express sexuality – would I venture to say joyous as well – by living and behaving in such a way as to completely free its followers from the stress factors ordinarily linked to sexuality.

Quebec is home to this incredible empowerment movement which characterizes one of the freest societies in the world.

It is therefore quite easy to understand why so many people want to enjoying surfing away from illnesses and specific cancers related to inadequate genital sexuality – often associated with E. coli – or related specifically to contraceptive practices.

Fundamental questions need to be asked in the face of such resistance towards the freedom to love: how do groups of people who blithely force their fellow human beings to procreate quite shamelessly, address their right to impose? Where do they really stand regarding the billions of children who suffer and are now asking them to be accountable?

In such a coercive environment who takes responsibility for the children who are or will be born? How do you explain to children what the real circumstances are surrounding their birth, and why they were neglected?

Why give birth, when you cannot correctly fulfill the responsibilities that are required of it, and when the children that are born are forced to live in such great distress? It is perhaps the most important question to ask in these horrendous times.

My interpretation of the meaning of the Shakespearean question "to be or not to be", is completely linked to the recurring question "to procreate or not". Because we have always thought, that we could "have been born or not born" at this very minute. We think of a blessed moment when lovers, long ago – our creators – were on the brink of choosing between two paths; to procreate or simply to meet each other with great simplicity and be rooted in the sacred energy… Did they have a choice or not? Only if they live in a country where people's freedom of choice still exists and is respected.

Intelligence and responsibility are at the root of wisdom. So it is easy to agree, that in certain circumstances, it is a very wise decision to walk away from pregnancy and know how to avoid contact between the semen and the ova. The plight of potential children is in our hands and of course we possess all the virtues to experiment with reproductive freedom.

In our great country, the liberation movement and the Quiet Revolution – which started in the 50's – and continued throughout the 60's and 70's – continues to inspire us and provide us with numerous opportunities to create the best conditions to ensure optimal living conditions.

We overturned the established order that wanted everyone to be submissive and we created a new order of discipline and of understanding Love. That is why we are very powerful at protecting our value system – as reflected in our political system, our democracy and our civil and criminal codes –, versus theocracy or other totalitarian political order.

As a generation who has witnessed submission, and subsequently freedom, let us continue to choose freedom.

When talking about freedom, physical security is extremely important, especially when it concerns the real distinctions between femininity and masculinity. It is clear the information related to this notion is somewhat inappropriate.

As an example, for the good of the cause, let's talk about a very distinctive part of the human body, its morphology and function that is all too often incorrectly depicted: the vaginal orifice. In fact, we were surprised to see the reproduction of the orifice in question and its vaginal cavity made of transparent plexiglass on a gynecologist's desk, and wrongly portrayed as an open cavity, 4cm wide, when in reality the cavity walls completely touch each other.

Yet, this important part of the female anatomy appearing to be more of a mold for the male sex instead of showing off its real nature convinced me that an indoctrination process was underway whereby the female sex was almost exclusively destined to be filled.

Herein lies a good part of the controversy and disagreement – and all the problems associated with it – that is, the reproductive characterization of female and male organs. The imagery linking these organs together falsifies reality for the sole benefit of copulation.

By its very nature, the vaginal and uterine cavities are closed, thus protecting their intimacy. During the feminist movement, the body was declared irrevocably inviolable – when rape was officially criminalized – in the last century.

At the time, in order to distinguish between this form and other forms of sexual assault, and because of its unique feature of being linked to the broad theme of reproduction, we considered that the term "rape" was really forced penetration with an actual or virtual link to possible impregnation.

In addition to the sacred nature of the intimate feminine temple, its vulnerability to diseases was also an issue.

So we ask ourselves the following question: is it really possible for anyone who does not pay special attention, to skillfully make their way into delicate feminine areas without causing harm? The openings being so close together puts them in a consistent and extremely precarious position to each other? And the other, – last, but not least – the anus, which is just as closed, and where there is a risk of ultimate and fatal outcomes if it is penetrated.

Is this being taught? Having observed the shocking incidence of sexual diseases, the answer is clearly no. Our opinion polls clearly show that most people have difficulty taking this problem into consideration or they reject its potential veracity.

It is not uncommon to see nowadays people being in total denial when it comes to admitting there is a possible correlation between the E. Coli bacteria and vaginal or urinary, urethra, uterus, prostate, kidneys, throat or stomach infections, or any other inner organs, for both genders combined that can be affected by the bacteria and its derivatives.

In the fifties, we detected and labelled patients who had acquired the bacteria as being people who went beyond the rules of good hygiene practices, and conversely, today, it's the people practicing a healthy sexuality that are sometimes ostracized, infantalized, ridiculed, or completely left out!! In heterosexual or homosexual relationships, you are ostracized if you refuse to submit to the penis intromission principle – or put some kind of object – into any of your orifices, and you are often cast aside for this, whether you are a woman, a man or an intersex person, and it doesn't take long before you are told to make an appointment with a health care professional or a sexologist who will try to argue with you and try to convince you that you are abnormal, and offer to treat you with tons of medication so that you rid yourself of your pseudo-sickness!!!

However, it is quite legitimate to feel discomfort when the act of penetration is mandatory, and in my humble opinion, it is quite commendable. It would also be advisable to consider that asking yourself questions about the reproductive process is a sign of higher intelligence concerning potential sexual problems, a greater awareness of human biology, a subtle sense of responsibility and a profound respect for the copulation process in all its greatness.

I want to say that I am not trying to prove that heterosexual couples are necessarily influenced by dictatorship, quite the contrary, since relationships, of any sort, in a free society, also deserve to be considered ecological. We have to be very careful in order to distinguish between encouragement to adopt a certain behaviour, that is the f/m relationship, and death threats aimed at compelling a person to comply. That is two different things.

Introducing objects into body cavities is a subject deserving special attention. At one year old, very early on, children must be made aware that branches, sand or other objects must not be inserted into their cavities. It is vitally important!!! Parents teach their children this.

We have received testimonials from young children who were asked to insert an object inside them. They talked about small wood branches inserted into sensitive and intimate areas of their body during discovery games or under other circumstances. They were, of course, strongly opposed to it.

I am sure you will agree: the simple fact that it is so hard for us to constantly repeat how important it is to handle problems of intrusion with delicacy, which never stops being a problem by the way, is one of the most shocking truths of humanity.

Chapter 20

Intrusion

While we're on the subject, I would like to humbly expose my point of view on the blatant ignorance regarding human orifices and as expressed sometimes in world media.

Let me recall the circumstances surrounding an insightful event which made front page news for months in 1998, when the conduct of the president of the United States was made public, but where he himself seemed to be ignorant of the problematic while having a possible intimate relationship with a young woman at the time when the story was made public throughout the entire world.

From a reliable source, it seemed that Mr. President had attempted to introduce a cigar into the sacred orifice of his current partner.

People who smoke cigars know that the Havana tobacco juice is very strong in the mouth, is that not so? And on the skin...it can be irritating and bring on an unpleasant burning sensation.

So can you imagine our surprise when we learned that the president himself had this sexual fantasy, and even worse, that he carried it out! Clearly, he did not take into account the fact that cigars give off highly irritant substances and potential contaminants, especially when it concerns an intrusion into a woman's holy orifice.

Whereas the phallic shape of the cigar seemed to attract global media attention, a much more disturbing factor was the sordid intrusion into the woman's sacred part. Indeed, this legendary and vile activity was a serious threat and could directly endanger the health of said person.

The toxic liquid that comes out of a cigar can cause much physical damage when introduced into the human body. But what exactly do we know about the physiological reactions in a woman's body, when objects are introduced "vaginally"? Certainly, if we rely on Health Canada statistics, 70% of people are affected by pains associated with questionable sexual practices.

Were you dreaming, or does this mean 70% of people do not worry about what is introduced into their bodies??? And speaking of this, "who" introduced "what", and "where"?? Well, let's talk about it.

To refute the idea that penetration is essential, another person interviewed told us:

"I remember fondly, during my childhood, profound moments when I felt a very strong libido, especially while playing with my friend at the time. One day, I remember quite well, we felt free and very close, and I was astonished to find I had reached what some

would call, an orgasm. There had been no touching. Only looks, words, in a moment of trust. I was clothed and so was my friend, I was standing up, simply living a private and joyful moment in my life, honestly, and in a very humane way."

Similarly, a talented writer who often participated in meetings during the feminist movement pointed out that her son had a very healthy behaviour: "*He has an erection when he laughs*".

This is very explicit, and it encourages the idea that intimate and personal pleasure depends, all things considered, on how much joy is created and felt at a given moment. No gestures and no touching are necessary for the body to be in a state of ecstasy! This is a revelation, no, it's a celebration which confirms that real or virtual gestures of love, when performed skillfully, and according to the Ecological Love theory, are a real "blessing".

It's not any more natural to enter a branch into a container than it is for a penis. Too bad, it is still inserted into infectious parts... It doesn't always have to have a cavernous destination as dictated by official society. The universe is infinite and offers to receive it with grace. Space is freedom. Semen greatly benefits from being released into the infinite universe.

Then, and only then, when there is consent as to the willingness to be impregnated, should the semen majestically make its way to the sacred entrance, with the strength of its real significance, before continuing on towards the ova.

We know that contraceptive pills given to women are not 100% effective. It is a tenuous situation at best, and in cases of unwanted pregnancies, it's very difficult, when these incidents occur, to decide with whom lies the primary responsibility.

However, when it's the gallant man who decides to manage his semen responsibly, the situation changes entirely and power relationships become more equal and ecological.

In the 21st century Earth has welcomed her 7,228,099,254th human. With all the disasters happening on the planet today, it goes without saying that we are overpopulated. It would therefore be advisable to establish the necessary mechanisms so that every human being can reproduce at his or her own discretion, without being forced into it as is the case presently.

This book is suitable for those who believe in freedom and have a positive attitude in order to develop the necessary strength for the betterment of the world.

The important thing to realize now is to recognize globally that there are other models, just as honorable as the sacrosanct f/m model for life.

Time spent with another human being is filled with significance and magnetism: the quality more than the number of hours, days or years spent with another person should be favoured. Every human relationship warrants our attention, unconditionally.

Chapter 21

Ecstasy

For centuries, we have fine-tuned our legislation to ensure peace and wellness for every human being and allow for a state of ecstasy.

Many parameters are involved. For example, we have noticed, among other things, that when things are going well in our professional life, we are more inclined to be aroused. And when we are aroused, the state of ecstasy is easier to access.

How many of us are willing to look at the situation in a more...pragmatic way? Let us talk to each other on the "Ecological Love.com" website…

Here is an excerpt from a documentary:

"I remember my first intimate nights with another person. A huge bed in an older apartment, my partner had a thousand faces; I thought she looked fabulous. I was really impressed. She had founded a theatre company with a few colleagues. She invited me to join the group, on stage, and to create sound effects and music for

the show. I was really good at this. I could play violin, guitar, piano, accordion, trumpet, percussion instruments, everything.

This new situation was a triggering event leading to feelings of great joy and passion for me. I also want to mention that we ate in a very healthy way. And to add to this idyllic picture, she had invited me to be a member of Montreal's first organic food cooperative. This could hardly be more appropriate for a young 19 year old university student. I was in my element. It was a consecration!

And when it was time to go to bed, I was in an altered state: a dream life, the land of milk and honey, where I could finally feel lustful! I was gently taming the contact with another human body: its softness, its skin and tongue texture. It was amazing. But things were somewhat spoiled for me, when in the middle of it all she asked me to do more daring things... My spleen was completely squashed and my slow ascent, simply fizzled out. I still don't know what childish reason made me conform, on the spot, to the standard sexual behaviour model or at least what I understood it to be then.

Even though I thought her command was somewhat inappropriate and a little crude, I chose to obey. I also agreed because I wanted to "find out about this modus operandi" which mistakenly seemed to bring together most human beings on the planet: making love was presented as a series of sexual practices learned here and there, in books, photos and films. I obeyed in spite of my convictions, even though I thought myself to be master in Tantric yoga! – an unwavering sign of my early appreciation of inner, slower and profound feelings –.

I obediently continued to follow my feelings harmoniously, in the role of an intrigued lover inspired by my sweet companion, by life itself, by my life, by nature, and of course, like a number of my compatriots by impregnation, birth, and also by my own conception and why not, by breastfeeding as well.

But deep down inside I am a fervent advocate of "the here and now" and my whole body was vibrating under a shower of pleasure in the presence of both our bodies and this sensual experience. Then there was the love juice!!

I remember all of it today, and I feel like starting over again precisely at the moment where I left my spleen, 37 years ago. At last, to live life the way I want! I have also realized that it is completely legitimate to prefer pure and simple relationships founded on trust and safety. I finally understood – albeit belated, but still – that the desire to live according to ecological, healthy and well-being principles, is more than honourable."

The lessons we have learned from this experience speaks volumes: even in today's homosexual behaviours, as with any mental imagery associated with sexuality in general, it appears partners are being pushed into reproductive practices, even though they have the best intentions in the world.

Another person told us:
"This is exactly what concerned me the most about my first sexual experience. I expected, rightfully, to have a slow, creative, tender and appreciative sexual experience. When one speaks of freedom, does it go all the way there as well? All the way, onto a straw, a rose, or a fern covered bed or even a bed covered with everlasting flowers! Has dictatorship overtaken my bedroom? Is there too much conformity? What an outrage! I want my more ethereal vision to be accepted..."

And we must admit that such comments about the need for peace and respect are quite numerous.

Chapter 22

Trickery

Trickery here is palpable. There is every reason to believe this great ongoing social adventure was set up when certain powers were usurped and some people coveted a population increase in their village when they figured out how profitable it would be for them!

For example, increasing "cheap" workforce availability and watching the tax collection pie increase can certainly be a great motivator, but the means used to do this are too often coercive and never properly carried out!

One must be quite corrupt to think of conspiring to increase a population through coercion! To keep people under the thumb of tyranny! Using tools made for hunting – guns, bombs, etc. – to impose power on the masses!!! Thinking of doing and even going ahead with this is very insensitive. It is most likely the work of mentally disturbed people who use psychotropic substances. It can be a royal couple, a family of notorious villains, or other pseudo-political associations, others, industries, everyone… One thing for sure, they are coercing entire nations as we speak.

I have been immersed for too long in humanist culture since my childhood, not to have a problem with the spirit of conquest. It is no secret, that some ideologies advocate the standardization of populations. There are dictatorships that have already built empires in the world. Some of those who hold power visibly want to gain ground and invade populated territorries…by enforcing reproduction. It is a widespread and totally observable global phenomenon. To all appearances, this coercion is inordinately insidious…

Will we be able to determine and insist loudly that "enforcing reproduction is a humanitarian crime"? Will the representatives of peace-loving countries be able to finally say: its "illegal here"? Will the international tribunal be able to rule soon on the compulsory nature of intercourse by admitting it is a completely unethical act on this planet?

In order to force people to reproduce, dictators use force, violence and terror. Females, males and intersex people are all equally subjected to this horror!

In many cases, people will have to, albeit unwillingly, form couples in order to reproduce according to a model in which even the number of children has been prescribed.

In democratic societies this dictatorship continues senselessly to exert its hold on the birth rates of some communities who persist in living quite shamelessly under a theocratic system, well-anchored in their culture, and end up with the obligation to give birth to three, eight and sometimes up to twelve children.

That is exactly what happened in Canada, or to be more precise, in Quebec, during the first sixty years of the last century, under the command of the catholic religion – jansenism and other faiths –, who were in close liaison with the state. While France, at the same time, was just breaking free from this situation.

Another one says:
"The number of pregnancies my mother had was staggering...She said she was in a lot of pain during her deliveries. As children, we were in a daze and depressed because of our scanty means of subsistence. So, out of the blue, we rolled up our sleeves, put our shoulders to the wheel, our shovels to the mortar, our trowel to the plaster, our brooms to the road, our hatchet to the aspen, and our straw in the barn to courageously earn our pittance."

Another related the following:
"We are strong and very aware. This evening, for example, I was watching a French film, like thousands of others that exist, in which a man hastens to open his fly, grasp his penis and brutally forces it into the vaginal orifice of a lady he hardly knows and for which he suddenly develops a crush!!! The young beauty is mortified, physically and morally and what is so appalling is that she can also become pregnant... I have been haunted by this scenario my whole life."

The aggression shown in an almost matter-of-fact way by the filmmaker is completely absurd according to the humanist point of view.

How many people have ever felt the indelicate nature and scope of this act practised here almost unconsciously? Yet, this daily practice has become common for some; even though it has far-reaching consequences – while the silence surrounding the scope of this practice is quite disconcerting –.

One has only to look at how young people struggle bravely through this: a tragedy is being played out, but its subject remains prohibited...Once again, the act of love takes on a new dimension when we encourage genitors to manage their own semen.

The current thinking on demography and the power we have over it is well underway. The older people remember having played out this scenario, written just for them, when during disastrous moments, the joy of living gives way to profound sadness, excruciating pain, severe irritation or chronic infection, herpes here, herpes there, and the pregnancy which may befall the oh, so young and innocent people born themselves to naive parents. So the birth of billions of pure children will have made and still makes big businesses very happy, as they merrily declare:

"Lot's of cheap labour, bring it on!"

During a romantic evening, the lovers only wanted to take care of and be kind towards one another. And surprise, surprise, impregnation and an unplanned pregnancy may result as a consequence of a genitally-oriented sexual practice imposed as the only type of relationship.

Who protects young people against this kind of situation? Who provides information to the young and old alike on the consequences of risky behaviours? It's a question of communication between us, and news travels fast!! Parents often find it difficult to talk about sexuality and the sensitive nature of the situation, when living proof of the consequences of their actions is standing right in front of them asking many questions, wanting clarification, for a real confrontation between genitors and their children.

Fourteen years old is such a young age to start taking birth control pills, medication and other things that potentially have unpleasant side-effects such as abdominal pain, depression, dizziness, headaches, hair loss, nervousness, etc., etc. There is often the formation of blood clots that can lodge themselves in the brain, heart, lungs, eyes and legs, as well as blindness, vomiting, fainting and speech problems....The information related to the taking of birth control pills is quite prodigious! We are asking of the too young patient to make decisions and take care of the situation, according to her circumstances or physiological predispositions...

Isn't this terrible and totally unacceptable for a developing teenager? And to take the pill on a daily basis at a specific time, supposedly to make sure it works... What a serious responsibility, what an ungrateful task!!! And all of this happens in order to perform so-called sexual intercourse! Oh, what fun! No thanks! And is pleasure guaranteed? Are you sure?

Fortunately, children born in the middle of the last century have more and more knowledge about certain intimate behaviours and the risk they pose to health. They can also detect the recklessness with which their own parents have behaved in this matter, as they were forced into a task imposed by a subtle diktat.

However, let's be careful. I would never presume to hold parents responsible for not having known any better. Neither should they be held responsible for having been themselves victims of threats or ploys by governing authorities. For example, they might have been indoctrinated or regimented, into developing an absolute confidence towards the rapid development of chemical pharmacopoeia over the past decades, while completely denying the existence of botanical medicine and being close-minded to any kind of inventory drawn up of the principal plants and their therapeutic use.

Fortunately, in many democratic societies this isn't the case anymore, the natural products industry is quite incredible.

However, we must pay particular attention to a time that has not completely gone by. Today, one only has to see how dictatorships continue to exist and interfere with democratic political systems in certain areas around the globe as they use educational tools that propagate teachings that promote violence between human beings, homophobia, etc…

Dictatorships are surely the horrifying consequences of the mental disorders of their leaders. Excessive behaviours can be linked to the possible intake of dangerous substances such as synthetic drugs, sleeping pills, anxiolytics and antidepressants which produce significant side effects. As well, many substances sometimes have undesirable effects like sugar, alcohol, coffee, all kinds of pills for blood pressure, and others, which act directly on the central nervous system and the sense of perception, in a very strong way.

It seems to be the only intelligent explanation when trying to explain the inconsistency of certain statements made by dictators which can be heard now and again in our immediate environment, and around the world. We only have to think of the madness shown by our dear friend Russia this year where apparently half the population was opposed to friendship between same-sex persons. Isn't it atrocious?

In the first place, how can you identify a person's sex in public spaces? Is it by the hair length or the clothes that don't correspond to the ones assigned to your gender? What are they? What uniforms are assigned to one or the other? Who decides what appearance should belong exclusively to one gender rather than another? Particularly when short dresses, long hair and high heels work equally well for all genders!

From a sociological and ecological point of view, how does one interpret the intentions of authorities who severely punish demonstrations of affection between two loving people?

Even if intimacy, sensitivity or sentimentality become part of friendship aren't its limits within each person's conscience? Friendship is a global phenomenon, and a friendly hug can have an intimate component to it in various degrees, depending on the situation and the relevant players.

Who wants to interfere between two people who appreciate each other and dictate the limits of their most intimate feelings?

Comments were made about these concerns. The most common was: "Leave us in peace". This is probably an indication that the time has come to clarify everyone's position on human relationships about sexuality in order to promote more meaningful and ecological teachings.

This is what we observe in groups where young people want to follow a pure and simple path in their friendly and intimate relationships – with same or different sex persons – and when they clearly want to embrace healthy and crystal-clear behaviours. They want to focus their awareness on themselves, their souls, and the universe in which they are living.

These young people no longer follow the old model when everyone else was driven to imitate others. They want to know, to learn, to think and anticipate the possible impact of their behaviours. They are interested in assessing their effects, their feelings and their pleasure, they want to avoid pain and recognize their real or fabricated longings and those they understand and adopt. Everything that seemed confused and secretive suddenly becomes clear and finally reveals itself. This ecological mouvement continues at a breathtaking rate everywhere, among people, friends, close or distant relatives.

Chapter 23

Natural Health

In light of natural health experiences and the wonderful virtues of medicinal herbs and their derivatives, clay and stone therapy, etc., and self-health practiced by a large number of people, it is clear that spitefulness does not have its place in a healthy mind and body. Human beings who follow a healthy diet, and occasionally use natural remedies, are more inclined to seek happiness. It is sheer joy, filled with generosity, intelligence, even genius, openness, ingenuity and sharing. This is what a healthy person feels like and this is what motivates her life choices. And, if any, she will remain true to herself throughout any therapy she decides to undertake.

While some consider that humans are prone to evil, my own evolution into the foray of natural health and self-health by the use of plants, etc., and having met other people who have taken the same path, has helped me to understand human history in a completely different perspective.

It is also clear that all human troubles, foibles and stupidities actually appear as being quite harmless, but they can also be the terrible consequence of having swallowed something bad...And all rifts and struggles are the painful repercussions of having swallowed poison...

In order to prove this, we can easily go back in time, during bloody conflicts.

So wouldn't it be worth it to establish strict controls on the consumption of substances for national leaders, so as to guarantee a more globally ethical and just space on earth? Just as we do in the fight against doping and its detection for competing athletes!

Another interesting question arises: is the quality of sperm compromised when its genitors swallow certain substances? The responsibilities carried by male and female genitors are admittedly great and quite important in terms of the quality of human beings they create, but also if their previous and current responsibilities are met. Also important, are the previous responsibilities of their own male and female genitors.

This is so much bigger! Of course, it goes far back or far ahead! The responsibilities attached to procreation are of the utmost importance. To have the power to create behaviours that have consequences – is considerable. This power has made us into who we are. And so, what we become as a civilization belongs to us. We also have the power to change an undesirable situation and decide to correct it, to purify or at least try everything to purify ourselves. Never stop trying, all the time, at the individual and collective level. Anyway, isn't this one of the foundations of freedom?

We have tons of evidence of personal rehabilitation cases, as this one:

"She had enough of being under the influence of alcohol, so she left with her friends to go into the woods and restore her health. She thought it would take six months, but it was really more like fourteen years. Fourteen years of hard work, and delight at seeing herself getting better, pushing the restart button and recovering the blueprint quality. It worked."

It also works very well at the social level. The transfer is quite impressive. We have not been put on earth to confine ourselves to restricting, constricting, controlling or restraining roles.

I have found the proof in this example, whereby, after having survived the horrors of the Second World War and its dreadful aftermath, we saw how the people of Quebec succeeded in breaking the chains put in place by the authorities. During a few troubled years, authorities tried to confine them to a rigid oath of obedience in relation to the enforced reproduction diktat. Commandments to which the majority responded by organizing protests and positive actions towards their autonomy. In the arts as well, so many inspiring individuals, holding strong and long-standing values and determined to be free, have helped to establish a new societal order and give us access to freedom. No sooner said than done.

Thus, in spite of the unimaginable harshness of its climate, this land, this territory, still bears the seal of wisdom and of the great power of love. Who would have believed it? Only by pure feelings and longings can these human beings have had access to the transcendental joys freedom brings!

Here again is someone else's testimony from a nearly outdated period, where a very young female felt embarrassed and thwarted in her scientific ambitions because she was obliged to wear unsuitable outfits to say the least:

"Even before the age of two, I angrily removed the stupid little dress where my behind was visible to everyone. I hated to be humiliated and my behind stared at constantly and ridiculed by my aunts and uncles. I felt like a martyr caught in a system in which I was a victim, deeply shaken and highly traumatized by a treatment I felt was inhuman and indecent.

When I took off my dress, with its stigmatizing effect, I was suddenly free from prison, hell, torture and dictatorship. I got through it like some of my friends by smashing the psychological barriers of conformity. I also escaped this straightjacket in early childhood, by experiencing ecstasy in the woods, where no one could disgrace us. As if suddenly, I was being raised by wolves. Thanks to the sensitive complicity of my tough girlfriend, my travelling companion who was two years my senior. We sometimes remained in the forest for half-days at a time; the force of nature, inspiring the very best of human virtues in me.

Afterwards, I always continued to search for a sense of justice, of truth and humanism. Dressed in trousers and sturdy shoes, I could roam the world; in the neighbourhoods around my house at first, then on to other distant lands."

Once again, the vibrant reality of this monograph account wields a powerful blow. The truth is neither to the left nor to the right, it's directly in front of us, like the cutting edge of a blade falling in the middle of everything.

Let us listen to another small part of a child's story, a child who has grown up and is only expressing her legitimate point of view. A point of view that one would think is coming from a human being buried under her experiences and who only wants to share, in her own voice, her convictions and her findings, with those who let themselves be loved.

"...A flash of inspiration made me see that the world was cut in half. On one side there are those who will reproduce and on the other, there are those who will experience their own unique life."

Sure enough, those who procreate have their own set of new dynamics in which they engage freely, as we can see in our countries today.

On the other hand, the pressures perverting the equality between alternatives prevent us from having the right to exercise freedom. There are intimidations and threats made through countless sarcasms and negative judgements towards friendship between same-sex persons. As a result, this possibility is promptly eliminated from possible life choices. This regrettable outcome is fatal for both the afflicted individual and society as a whole!

Chapter 24

Libido

We have graciously gathered the following comments:
"Oh, I sympathise very much with people diagnosed as having sexual dysfunction, especially when they decide to take certain so-called harmless prescribed medicine with unfortunate side effects...

For example, conventional medicine describes some treatments for erectile dysfunction as causing redness on the face, headaches, etc.... Other medicines like birth control pills, antihistamines and antidepressants, can also cause cancer, as well as dry-up the vaginal mucosa in some women...

Suddenly, just because you have a simple drop in libido, you find yourself with a red rash on your face, so, in my opinion, I'm convinced you have just destroyed what was left of the desire one may have had for you, or better still, you have destroyed your self-esteem and crippled what was left of your carnal passion!

Or worst still, you are in such a predicament, you suffer mental anguish of perhaps being diagnosed with cancer, caused by taking contraceptive pills or medication designed to control hot flashes, or you have mood swings associated with having taken pills with a high concentration or other synthetic psychotropic substances to cure your ills.

Perhaps it is medicine itself that is sick. Isn't it completely illogical to want to cure a pseudo-dysfunction by making it worse, all the while pretending to make it better? Just like marketing gimmicks that plague advertising messages, whereby one sells the opposite virtues of product x in order to sell the idea of using the product. In fact, if "x" creates stress, we are told it appeases. Like coffee, for example. We certainly agree that lying is not a rule in the retail industry, it is a huge swindle, a pointless strategy which pollutes our environment and is a waste of our time and resources."

Sexuality and libido are very subtle and personal matters, and it is generally recognized – joyfully we hope – that the demanding nature of these characteristics in the human body is experimented with a high degree of sensitivity.

We all know libido has its own internal fluctuations capable of inspiring us to get close to someone or to distance ourselves from one another. Sometimes our libido can be at its lowest and remain there during a number of months and even years. In which case, depending on our situation, we can choose to investigate the causes of our decreased sex drive, whether it is physical, psychological, spiritual, economical, familial, social or other. But still, isn't this drop in libido just perfectly normal under the circumstances?

Experience has shown that the quality of our libido depends on the state of our physical, sentimental, spiritual and emotional health, even our social situation, financial health, the progress of our projects and our joys, open communication, etc.... And the belief we are fulfilling our dreams…

To succeed in fulfilling only part of a dream will often be enough to create an atmosphere leading to sensual pleasure.

Throughout our lifetime, we have a duty to choose solutions that will bring us joy. Isn't our goal to enjoy life? We just need to follow our inner voice to feel its magnificence! Our goal will lead us to achieving an intelligent and quiet self-actualization process without rushing.

There is no need to artificially boost – by means involving the risk of undesirable side effects, for example –, the inner strength that comes with the joy of loving and of being loved. It comes from being in great shape, eating well, and doing exercises and stretches, facing the moon or the sun, and respecting our own rhythms and dance movements. Just having freedom of movements can lead to an increased libido.

In an atmosphere where one is conscious of one's own vitality, knowledge of sublimation is a must. Indeed, sublimation is a great practice to manage your libido and generate a multitude of benefits that we will talk about more in depth in our next volume, *Ecological Love: The Practice.*

To work hard, to feel our qualities and our strengths, to recognize our skills and accomplishments; all of this is crucial if we want to experience our sensual pleasure.

When we dig a canal in the mud to keep the water flowing, pack down leaves or rocks so that a pool, even a very small one, is formed, screw down a board, sweep a very cluttered basement,… all of this can lead us to sensual pleasures and should be welcomed gracefully; and in turn, will help us manage our projects and our actions.

To study a contract, write clauses, verify information about a real estate property, work the land and photograph it from a helicopter. Work hard. Pay for a tool, a machine, a printer, a car. Paint, shoot a film, write, draw, sing. Everything is a reason to be passionate, and so, we continue to do what we do well.

Is beauty a mix of attitude, feelings and health…? Doing what we must do to make our bodies beautiful is a must. The bright colours of the sun will reflect its beauty. Take time to walk, or lie down dressed in light clothing or naked to give your skin the desired texture…

In a democracy, the right to nudity is totally accepted and is essential for many people. However, some theocracies vehemently condemn it; it is a very controversial subject among people.

In countries where sovereign power lies with the people, it is undeniably a challenge for everyone, to make sure they do everything in their power to reach the highest levels of happiness, in particular through the knowledge and application of the laws of being. Getting the most out of life, today!

But beware, there is one major difficulty… Although we want to experience life in all its aspects, something else is happening today: human poverty has taken on such proportions that we can no longer ignore it.

Many of us feel they have literally been taken hostage here. Yes. Even though many people are valiant, talented, conscientious, and work hard, they never seem to reach a state of human dignity; unfortunately they live in substandard living conditions, below the poverty line.

They are deprived of food, lodging, clothing and safety. Too many of us come from a background where we were often neglected during our childhood years. So – since no one takes pleasure from human poverty or from the distress of others which continues to grow – we are really trying to understand the cause of such a dreadful state of affairs that has already reached is peak.

Chapter 25

Resources

We can often feel trapped by the very fact our own birth is the result of a colossal sham.

In the middle of the last century, over several decades, many populations – especially in Quebec – reproduced at an outstanding rate, apparently obeying mandatory commands, and were totally in bondage under a subtle, underlying and increasingly apparent dictatorship. So be it.

This high birth rate might just be consistent with other more ephemeral necessities. We can always give ourselves the benefit of the doubt. So be it. We are alive. But insofar as the future of humanity is concerned, we obviously have the opportunity to regulate its performance the best possible way, and to chart a way forward towards empowerment.

The demographic curve has been growing exponentially quite drastically, for more than 200 years now. In the millions of years before, there may even have been a decline or a stagnation period in population growth. Not always caused by famine or other disasters such as war crimes, as so many people like to think, but is simply the result of totally respecting individual integrity which leads to a more harmonious, clear and real geographic distribution, in harmony with the natural laws surrounding the freedom to reproduce, when the act of mating doesn't become an obsession. Certainly it could also lead to a better and more organic and just distribution of wealth in which we have the freedom to reproduce or not, and if appropriate, whether we leave a more or less sizable inheritance to our offsprings.

No one is despicable enough to want a child to be born into poverty. Any personal and informed decision on our part is essentially a conscious and intelligent one to protect ourselves and to ensure that we have the best possible survival conditions. People who are forced to reproduce testified they had to obey this command under threat of torture. And even during our investigations in Asia and Africa, people have testified to the fact they were forced to copulate, even against their will, and uttered death threats by certain groups. Some people even told us that their freedom to act was literally taken away from them, and that their existence was fully dedicated to these torturers who had stolen their freedom of choice.

The compelling story of a woman from Quebec, just one of many, who would have had nine pregnancies between 1943 and 1964 under the dictatorship of the powers that be, terrorized she would have burned alive in hell for having prevented the family! It only took one night of insubordination to undergo this dreadful ordeal.

"To be sure, if I had let my husband ejaculate on my lower thigh without forcing him all the way into my cavity, I would have been excommunicated and be allowed to burn in hell forever."

It's terrible to think free ejaculation was prohibited in Quebec! It shows to what extent the madness was then.

Nonetheless, citizens were lied to over and over, thanks to a rigorous curriculum taught in various provincial teaching establishments, with the added bonus of cultivating poverty.

To the people who belonged to a church or a state that were all-powerful for a brief period of time, this was the kind of hogwash they continually heard all around them. Then, around the middle of the sixties, a rapid decline of this hegemony that had lasted for nearly 20 years, from the Second World War, where so many horrors had provoked, among the general population, the fear of not being able to break from the orders given by belligerent conquerors: the fear of reprisals and the fear of punishments reserved for the rebellious ones.

And those so aptly named the baby-boomers are the fruits of this organized terror.

Yes, we talked a lot about the baby boom period! But, to date, have we totally escaped from it? Maybe. In any case, one thing is certain, people have reflected on the matter, and then challenged the powers that be, rising through concrete like flowers pushing through the gravel! The Quiet Revolution occurred and a new state of mind oriented towards more humane values was born.

During the substantial and complete reform of the education system, school texts and other educational materials were stripped of their sexist language. In today's context, where the quality of education is a determining factor, and when values to be transmitted correspond to a certain democratic utopia, it is extremely important to continue this work and strip sexist language from books, other audiovisual documents, etc., that are coming from other countries, some of them being theocracies, so that any educational material used will be more relevant to the education of newcomers entering free zones.

Even though much progress has been made after the quiet revolution, when taking a closer look at people's intimate behaviours today, we are astonished to discover the persistence of timeless remains from a bygone time.

Therefore, in an effort to improve the situation, it is our duty to correct any disparities in our will to live better, more prosperously, healthier, and thus happier. The edges of those disparities are perfectly patterned after the old behaviours of our predecessors, in a way that still strips us of our dignity, to the point where we risk loosing control of our own sensuality. Hard to admit, you say? And yet, we are convinced we hold the reins of our existence!

Speaking of which, it is more than urgent to question why in Canada we have such an audacious contradiction in the Constitution Act, 1982, namely, in the Canadian Charter of Rights and Freedoms, where it is solemnly declared, in the first line, that in addition to promoting the rule of law, Canada is founded on a principle that recognizes the "supremacy of God".

It is completely contradictory to talk about the supremacy of God in a democracy – its own definition being the sovereignty of the people – because that is what precisely distinguishes democracy from theocracy.

In a theocracy, divinity holds sovereignty – it is a system governed by religious people –. In short, the word **democracy** is a term that comes from the Greek and means "sovereignty of the people " and the word **theocracy** is a term that also comes from the

Greek and means “sovereignty of God”.

To correct this error – that has potentially disastrous consequences – we simply have to remove immediately the phrase “sovereignty of God” from the Canadian Charter of Rights and Freedoms document.

This is important, as it it precisely this “religious” concept which acts as a shield against laws which respect human rights.

At the UN, when representatives from theocratic countries enter into global agreements they always add the small phrase “except for our religious convictions”. Because of this exclusion, they claim that it is legitimate to commit incredible violence and acts of terror opposing celibacy, homosensuality, and even chastity, feminineness, and masculineness. In the face of such opposition to people’s virtues all over the World, this situation totally disregards the founding principles of the UN established specifically to develop friendly relations between nations, promote social progress, improve living conditions and increase respect for human rights.

> *The* ***United Nations Organization (UN)*** *is an international organization regrouping, with some exceptions, every country on the planet. Distinct from its member countries, the Organization’s purpose is to ensure international peace. Its objectives are to facilitate cooperation in international law, international security, economic development, social progress, human rights and achieve world peace. Founded in 1945, after the Second World War, to replace the League of Nations, stop wars between countries and provide a platform for dialogue. It contains several subsidiary agencies to help it complete its mission successfully. (Cf.* “*History of the United Nations*” *[*archives*]*, on *the official United Nations website* (website visit was made on February 14 2014).

Following this terrible mind game, we have to quickly address this issue as the race to populate the planet is creating a massive imbalance between the demographic representation of democratic countries and those from theocratic countries, where educational programs are totally centred around forced reproduction and its corollaries.

There are many sensitive human beings who are attuned to the universal vibrations and hear the call for peace, freedom, and faith in the human and cosmic human intelligence, and understand the significance of responsibility.

All the efforts that have been put into a healthy and responsible consumption bear fruits, when producers, production and distribution chains, etc., love the land and its natural resources for their divine energy.

Through this brilliant and passionate synergy between human beings and their environment, plants, water, fire, terrestrial magnetism and its endlessness, its known and unknown galaxies, a tremendous strength emerges from this great collaboration between the elements and also between human beings. In the end, all resources achieve balance peacefully, in an atmosphere of love. And for this to come true, each human being must be valued.

This is what has clearly emerged from a survey given to people from all walks of life.

And in case Canada wants to keep "the supremacy of God" principle in its laws – although the UN doesn't integrate it, and we understand why –, if push comes to shove, I am preparing myself to answer publicly about what God wants.

Part Five: *COMMITMENT*

Chapter 26

Sodomy

The strength of convictions encouraging freedom will certainly succeed in promoting the integrity of the individual, in response to the appeal made to all religious leaders to play a major role in the promotion of an interfaith and intercultural dialogue for peace.

In many cultures – religious or not – we face great dissension when it comes to homosexuality, so I had to devote special attention to find the possible causes of certain dispositions towards homosexuality. It seemed that the same logic applies here when we know that the ultimate aim of totalitarian societies is to create cheap labour, increase the number of consumers that will buy a variety of products like cars, pills, and many more, and where forced reproduction is the norm.

To achieve these aims, we have observed the following: gender polarization – denial of the existence of intersex people – the disagreement around clothing, which varies according to gender so as to force the identification of the genders and oblige people to associate, according to the "f/m" scenario, as well as assign them to a strictly reproductive sexuality where penetration is at the heart of the act.

This way of operating is integrated within the education curriculum and influences everyone's intimate behaviours; it can even influence people who have homosexual relationships. The diktat is so deeply engrained in our behaviours that it inevitably tells us that intimate relationships necessarily include penetration – it is in fact the norm – into any one of the available orifices.

It is the only plausible reason for sodomy to exist, we don't know who practices it, and even though it is inherently unclean, it is still practiced with a totally apparent disregard for the basic understanding of human biology!

It is precisely the worst fault attributed to homosexual relationships. However, our research has shown that same-sex lovers often do not operate this way. They are rather opposed to the penetration model, and in fact choose to dissociate themselves from this type of behaviour. They also say that in most situations where they know sodomy is present, it has more to do with people who usually engage in heterosexual relationships who propose buggery – which, by the way, is perceived as not being very popular: the real consequences of these anal games are increasingly well-documented –.

So, for anyone who prioritizes health, there is no doubt that the practice of sodomy is the outcome of an appalling deception.

However, we have sometimes noticed that a great number of people, however well-intentioned, have repeated this behaviour.

Let's take the example of two men who want to be close: why is there an existing myth that says men have to necessarily practice sodomy? Could it be because they have been so indoctrinated in putting their penis in an orifice, that they have found one on their own bodies.... But by no means the least: I call it the anus!

The filmmaker Pedro Almodovar presents this activity – namely anal penetration – as being completely natural in his film "*The Skin I Live In*".

We can even question whether or not he is trying to tell us how boring it is to have to penetrate your partner from behind without seeing his face or be able to exchange glances, or brush against his mouth or forehead. He seems to show impatience in the face of impotence! With great transparency, would he have barely scratched the surface of this important question about the quality of the orifices and the age-old question of penetration? Yes, he was definitely on topic; he hit the nail right on the head! He delivers quite candidly the essence of a practice that, in a sense, is still subjected to the diktat, insofar as it demonstrates a fascination with orifices.

During all our childhood we practice the basic rules of hygiene, but unfortunately, they go right out the window when current films and literature depict sodomy as only one "practice" amongst many others, while in relation to natural health, it appears to be a practice to be avoided at all costs, as it is highly unhealthy, is based on ignorance, and is frankly unacceptable, period.

In our quest for sanity it is a question of logic as we must first compare two of the available orifices in the human body and briefly assess their quality.

First, we will include in the competition, the orifice appearing between the thumb and index finger of a closed fist, a healthy orifice, a sacred and flexible orifice offered with such generosity and a loving and tender hand, to all those interested.

For your consideration and if a further argument is needed, this orifice is part of every individual, women, men and intersex persons.

Blessed is this orifice by which love can be expressed with a greater peace of mind. In fact, when we close our fist, we form a flower with our hand that extends and closes quite easily and is unlike anything else.

Secondly, not very far from the loving fist is the anal orifice... And if someone cannot tell the difference, he would only have to smell one and the other to see which of the two is the good one!

It is well known, that over time, and with the experiences and exchange of information in gay areas, more and more people are coming out and saying they prefer to have moments of shared pleasures, simply, without having to make contact with mucous membranes, through kissing, or partaking in high-risk genital activities. So, it goes without saying, to avoid playing with the anal orifice.

Ecological Love is a growing movement!!!

It is sheer happiness for the other, to never become a hostage, and where genders can meet frankly and honestly. It is the rise of true sexual freedom and the time to reclaim our bodies.

Chapter 27

Stress

The pseudo-liberation of the sixties and seventies is very different. It came about when the magic pill was introduced and was supposed to ensure the safekeeping of reproductive behaviours, but without the normal outcome of pregnancy, and with all those minor inconveniences, like not being 100% sure it would prevent gestation, and a side effect of potentially giving cancer! Wow! And all for the sole purpose of sharing a few moments of tender sensual pleasure? Really?

These uncertainties will only have succeeded in creating physical, psychological, spiritual and emotional stress…

Clearly, with the introduction of the birth control pill, one cannot speak of freedom when we witness such a disastrous enslavement process that has put off more than one person.

This can be nerve-racking for eighteen year olds who believe they are elegantly entering a world of love, when in fact they must first go through the door of a doctor's office to obtain their divine prescription! Meanwhile, the market for contraceptive pills is growing.

Fortunately, many do not want to adhere to this way of doing things. The movement for taking charge of your own body and health has made great strides, particularly in the marketing of countless natural products designed, with the best intentions in mind, in many countries around the world, to ensure optimal overall health.

It's fairly easy to understand that some national and multinational companies have carried out a large scale bluff around contraception because they draw real benefits from population growth and can, at certain times, exert pressure to that end. But why are people interested in obeying this scheme?

It is one thing for car manufacturers to see their profits go up because of a higher demand brought on by an increase in the number of consumers, but quite another, when we've now reached a point where we are loosing control of our own reproductive process.The high-level companies who accumulate wealth are the only ones benefiting from this situation, while a population reproducing itself this way, is less and less able to seek self-sufficiency.

Sociologically speaking, we could say that when people become richer at the expense of others, it could perhaps be everyone's fault.

The abundance of manpower – where individuals hardly have any family money, and as such are available to work in poorly paid jobs – is one person's progress and another's catastrophe.

Documentaries are full of images showing people working on machines, like ants, and complaining about the inhuman working conditions.

And there are those as well who are completely cut off from the workforce. How many people can boast of having pleasant living conditions? Wouldn't it be interesting to identify who they are and determine what their percentage is?

How does everyday life unfold in urban areas when methods are not immune to the diktat?

At youth gatherings or parties, for example, where sexists roles are relentlessly reproduced. Here again, the female-male duality is often not able to sustain reality or the truth… It often condemns a person to lie to herself or to others … or to lie to loved ones.

In certain respects, it can engender a painful situation, and it is clear that everyone suffers from these behaviours when they constantly have to make things up.

It is important to speak of such things in order to avoid the suffering that may occur in an environment manipulated by commercialism.

We can certainly claim that this debate is really taking place today in Quebec, perhaps more than anywhere else, because we allow ourselves to explore and live a life, where freedom of association and freedom to reproduce limits sexist behaviours and the stereotyping of human beings into roles where they slowly fall off the edge into powerlessness.

The human body is amazingly well made. It will thrive in the spirit of joy and peace. Love certainly does not need the intrusion of the pharmaceutical industry. And, if there is an infectious area in our body, let's take it into consideration. Is it asking for too much intelligence from sexologists and psychologists who still advocate for the practice of sodomy, fellatio and anilingus? Faced with this problem, sensitive human beings – even though they have been unjustly accused of modesty by those same sexologists and psychologists – continue to believe in the virtues of healthy and thoughtful behaviours.

What kind of universe are children being born into today?
"At the rate things are going, by 2025, half the children in the United States will be diagnosed with autism. Stephanie Seniff of the Massachusetts Institute of Technology (MIT) a panelist at the presentation of a study on the increase use of a weed-killer containing an active ingredient called glyphosate and the increasing rate of autism, made the public's hair stand on ends." Article published by Catherine Cordonnier, December 26th 2014, *http://www.topsante.com/medecine/medecine-divers/environnement-et-sante/un-enfant-americain-sur-2-pourrait-souffrir-d-autisme-d-ici-10-ans-74855* (In French only)
And if the human reproductive process is effectively influenced by strong interests, it's easy to believe that sleazy business people could adulterate products intended for human consumption. In a world where half the people are totally destitute, and suffer from misery, they bear witness to the fact that they cannot participate in the development process of which they are the unfortunate victims.

Let me quote our geologist and ecologist colleague François Gay:
"The rise in local and world population and the increase in consumption everywhere have created an imbalance so important that nature has not had sufficient time to renew itself, compensate for the loss of resources, and restore the previous situation." (see Article *Protégeons notre environnement: c'est urgent!* Journal de Bromont *Ici Maintenant*, déc. 2014/janv. 2015, Vol. 20. Num.6) (In French only)

As is well known, the scandalous cheap labour force surplus only benefits the capital of some people. You see it even today, when engineers and doctors rapidly become labourers in their respective areas of activity, employed by experienced firms who themselves are delighted to hire new prospects recently qualified from universities all over the world.

Since we have to decide what to do, would you advocate for love or for supernumerary? Quality or quantity, what do you prefer?

Are you for gays, and cheerfulness, that is the question of the day? This is the big question. France and Russia are our friends. But they are facing a terrible disaster: the indoctrination of their population to refuse gentleness between same-sex people. According to the latest information, a reign of terror exists in Russia and you cannot extract yourself from this harsh reality, especially if you are seen in the company of a same-sex person and appear to be close because you will be punished for it.

"As soon as ... one becomes openly gay, that's when the problems begin. As soon as one goes out into the public space, one is threatened."

http://www.lexpress.fr/actualite/monde/europe/russie-des-que-l-on-declare-ouvertement-son-homosexualite-on-est-menace_1321032.html#sFtoCo6W5UbJEyD5.99 *(In French only)*

A great many of us are not comfortable with intercourse and this is very interesting, sociologically speaking, when trying to evaluate the real percentage of people who desperately want the right to live alone, to live freely with a partner of their choice and their bodies to be respected.

Consider the example of two young people who are friends: it is incredibly pleasing. It glows with a tenderness that is pure wonder. A strong bond may develop. We understand quite well that they might, quite normally and naturally, have an increase in their libido, even without touching, and sometimes possibly at the same moment? Happiness is so present and foreseeable that it is no wonder their libido improves. It can even go higher and remain high for a certain time…isn't that so? I am not making this up.

What are the real implications and consequences of this relationship? Apart from the joys it brings, there does not seem to be any disagreeable aftereffects. Does the relationship have any consequences on their health? Clearly, it depends on the additional steps they might or might not take insofar as their sexual practices are concerned. If the two subjects decide to adopt the brutal and unrestrained genital model, yes, it is possible for their practice to be risky. Many sexual activities that are encouraged between all kinds of people imply erotic games involving rectal, vaginal, and oral orifices, etc., etc. That these activities are practised between same-sex people does not indicate it will put them at greater risk than partners of different genders, it is quite the contrary.

Conversely, it is possible for their relationship to be subtle, ethereal, and sensual without getting involved in genitality or bestiality, but involving a sense of soft voluptuousness without having to resort to unfortunate and painful exchanges. Everything happens on the exterior of the body, with much tenderness and understanding. Isn't this a more valuable alternative?... In any case, these behavioural choices should be made based on sound judgement and full awareness.

Had I heard of the *Ecological Love* concept in my childhood, I would have understood much earlier what healthy sexual desires were and thus would have been in a better position to choose more natural behaviours. Furthermore, knowing that there was a school of thought much closer to the way I thought about love, I would have had the necessary strength to defend the right that my desires and I should be respected.

This is intended to help young people make enlightened choices and achieve healthy behaviours in this regard: I wanted to ensure the development of an approach that seemed more adapted to the actual ambiguity pervading in the world about this.

In light of these considerations, the *Ecological Love* concept is worth knowing as a happy alternative and maybe, let's hope, as an replacement solution to the current model of forced intercourse, which fewer and fewer people in the world advocate.

Chapter 28

Myths

We can also see what happens in the gay community when there are false allegations made about gay men in that they are brutal and supposedly have all kinds of outlandish sodomy practices.

But, in light of the information gathered, we found it was mostly men in heterosexual relationships that initiate high risk penetration practices with other men that engage in such behaviours. Their spirit is most certainly marked and tormented by the degrading pseudo-obligation to penetrate.

As with any heterosexual relationship today, the obsession to penetrate can be so consuming for partners that they will do their utmost to explore all the nooks and crannies of the body – however small, to the point where they will enlarge them if need be (see fist-fucking and the rest) – in order to penetrate them.

Admittedly, we are totally sceptical when it comes to the percentage of women, men and intersex persons known to enjoy these types of intimate behaviours.

Many men eloquently testify of their discomfort when they have *doubtful* feelings during penetration of the vaginal canal. And there are countless number of cases where women have felt a similar discomfort during these supposedly routine activities…

During our research, we extracted information from specialized sources on the Internet which said that one third of people who practice fellation did not like it at all, while others claim that it is more like 50%.

Can we deduct from this that people are forced into these practices without their consent? What's happening? I'm not dreaming. Do these people engage in behaviours they do not like?

Chapter 29

Shadow and Silence

On the other hand, it is an unmistakable fact that there are numerous persons who desperately want to find a lover willing to share sensual pleasures, without having to participate in activities that turn them off. This new vision full of sensual pleasures is precisely making it possible for us to create a set of gentler practices that take into account the physical, emotional, spiritual and mental stability and overall health of human beings. Sweet love, it is the beginning of the recognition of the art of true love, sweet love, *Ecological Love*.

What are the practices routinely described and authorized today in magazines containing articles on sexology? Obviously those on reproduction as well as those on the never-ending question of penetration, with all its devices prescribed to enhance performance, condoms, lubricants, all of that … cunnlingus, anilingus, sodomy, and many more. The same thing seems to be stipulated for any relationships, even though forced genitality affects the integrity of any person who does not like to engage in these types of activities.

Of course, for all others, everything is hunky-dory. And for those who rebel – the gentle people – they are subjected to all kinds of threats if they do not conform to the cravings of others who firmly believe they are on the right side!

This unequal confrontation is precisely what motivates my reasoning. The hegemony of these do-gooders who ridicule and consider those gentle people as abnormal and marginal affects me deeply. In all of this, one really understands that it is the wishes of these mild-mannered people that are being trampled on. They are the ones who are routinely advised to go and see a shrink. They are the newly marginalised; they are left in the shadow, in silence.

This book represents the symbolic words of a person, one among many, who has been mistreated, – the accurate numbers are unknown at this time – to confront the unfair harassment of which we are the unfortunate victims. Request: that we grant to everyone the freedom to express their deepest and most intimate wishes!

And our numbers keep growing every day. Those of us who prefer to be physically healthy and are able to live a peaceful and voluptuous sensuality, without any artifice, medication, irritation, allergies, urinary or fecal matter mixed in with our smile, or other. We do not wish to convince, but only to achieve our rightful status, and a legitimate credibility to say the least! To live side by side in mutual recognition of one another, and to end torture and be savagely burned at the stake for wishing to love in a dignified and clean way. To stop undue pressures meant to enslave us and annihilate our intense and loving sex drives, and to destroy us, ravaged and overwhelmed as we are when having to face the never-ending nightmare of venereal diseases and of all kinds of cancers.

To address the notion of *Ecological Love* means to speak about a natural way of loving, a healthy way of loving. Why would love be a vector for disease? How does biology give us new insights into our relationships? Is medicine powerless or simply silenced, or is it just not allowed to convey vital health information in relation to today's sexual contacts? What specifically does it propose if not a full-range of synthetic medicines often with side effects worse than the immediate ones, even though they are intended to regulate the diagnosed dysfunction?

There has to be a way to flush out those who play the ostrich and stick their heads completely in the sand, and keep their ears burried as well.

"The scandal of 3rd and 4th generation birth control pills is only the first episode of what could be the biggest medical blunder of the 21st century."

Ref.: « La pilule contraceptive - Dangers et alternatives», Éditions Du Rocher, 2013. Professeur Henri Joyeux et Dominique Vialard (In French only)

Even though they aptly denounce the birth control pill scandal, Joyeux and Vialard's publication still tries to convey, albeit naively, the idea that penetration is treated as mandatory or at least is inevitable, thereby perpetuating this abominable situation. The authors never question the appropriateness of expressions of love as prescribed in our modern societies.

Equally terrible are the medical and biological laboratories' attitudes, whereby they seek solutions to ensure that women and men continue to take the necessary steps to procreate when there is effectively no procreation. This is no mean feat!! The very principle of impregnation is, well, totally overshadowed.

But who within the population is so intent on being involved in reproductive activities? Of course, there are those whose desire to conform is so strong, they firmly believe that these are *the only* socially accepted sensual activities for them – and that is where the problem lies – and the mere fact of refusing to participate in these activities is sufficient enough to be considered abnormal! This is a very tenacious delusion. It has never been seen before, "or has it"? It has never been seen, never been heard, never been lived "I can't take it anymore"!

At one point, it becomes totally ridiculous to always be confronted like this by our peers on this very touchy subject.

While there are more and more people who are quite satisfied with living simple and sensuous relationships, there are others who are more stubborn and inclined to practice the suggested genital activities and judge others as being inhibited, thus supporting the views expressed by dictatorships which prohibit and sanction any kind of pleasure – considered "unnatural" – in many parts of the world!

Oh, how the representatives of the dominant ideology in our civilisation seem to be numerous and well structured! For example, they label anyone who stays on the side of hygiene as being "childish". And since this is a sensitive issue, one does not wish to be seen as lacking audacity or maturity for "refusing" to practice a more genital sexuality, and therefore a more risky one. In the face of such aggression, many people comply and side with the overwhelming majority. "Pseudo-majority" – because it is legitimate to question this majority status –: in fact, how many conform themselves to this for fear of being labelled abnormal?

It is essential for the counting process to begin, given the urgency to know exactly how many people think it is of the utmost importance to practice a sensuality geared towards respecting their partner's health.

It is also essential to hear the comments of people who can attest to having been coerced in order to conform to a single model. This will give us the opportunity to challenge the false claim that sexuality is strictly a personal matter and that these intimate choices have nothing inherently to do with pressures of any kind.

Now is the time to take stock of this historical matter!

It is also time to address each others' cultural mores. I would like to revisit the example when the president of the United States put a cigar into his partner's orifice. Even though the gesture seemed innocent enough, it was completely reprehensible! One would have to be completely careless to do such a potentially harmful thing. Can you imagine the damage this can cause inside the body?... A liquid saturated with tobacco slowly making its way to the birth canal; do you believe this is a good place for tobacco to be? When we know that tobacco products can contain up to three thousand chemical substances of which 28 are carcinogenic!! All of this, inside the sacred temple of a woman's body… My gracious me…it is beyond the imagination! With the passage of time, what really happens inside the body of such a victim; inflammation, cancer, rot?....

It is worse than a simple humorous or naughty fact for many, when the cigar is just compared to a phallic object, among others. It is a highly criminal and condemnable act due to the severity of the illnesses it is most likely to cause. It would have been more useful if this disturbing fact had been mentioned in the publicity surrounding this event, that the principle to undermine the person's integrity and health be spelled out, and that the behaviour within this context, be denounced.

Chapter 30

Illnesses and Genitality

Another calamity: the human papillomavirus. According to Canadian statistics, HPV (human papillomavirus) is a sexually transmitted virus, or as we say, it "originates" from sexual practices – the issue of sexual *transmission* should not disregard the cause or suggest that it is only external, but should also include the fact that the concept originates from sexual practices, whereas sexually transmitted diseases can be caused by sexual contact during an intimate act – and is the most widespread virus in Canada and in the world.

According to our information and assessments, this type of infection can most likely occur *in situ,* for example, when the liquid from the rectal orifice is deposited in the vagina or the urinary tract.

"It is estimated that as many as 75% of sexually active women and men will have at least one anogenital HPV infection in their lifetime." (Health Canada Cf.: http://www.hc-sc.gc.ca/hl-vs/iyh-vsv/diseases-maladies/hpv-vph-eng.php.)

"Anyone who has had sex is at risk for HPV. It is therefore recommended to practice safe sex." http://www.hc-sc.gc.ca/hl-vs/iyh-vsv/diseases-maladies/hpv-vph-eng.php.)

According to these sources, since the virus can also cause cancers – such as uterine, vulva, penis, anal, mouth, throat and tonsil cancers, etc. – what safety practices are recommended? Vaccination, cancer screening, reducing the number of partners, condom use…

And I haven't even mentioned hepatitis B, AIDS, syphilis, gonorrhea, genital warts…

Let us say here, that in the book *Ecological Love: The Practice*, we will give detailed information on ways to get close to one another without causing harm to each other.

There is a vast amount of information on the subject of genital sexuality, but partners seem to favour the concept of neglecting and trivializing the responsible management of semen and of certain gender-related morphologies.

Certain official websites surprisingly persist in suggesting practices that do not visibly meet the highest standards of quality… Especially when your demands to be respected are met with warnings of violence on the part of your partner …like when you try to convince your partner to have safer sexual relations. Whoops, that is a tough playing field. And this comes from government sources… What is happening to the population at the present time? Do we think certain behaviours are normal when they are totally unacceptable?

At an early age, I was privileged to witness the work of a nurse who had set up an infrastructure to screen people for sexual diseases, together with the voluntary commitment of a very courageous doctor, in order to target diseased patients and seek their cooperation in disclosing the names of their partners, if appropriate. This happened in the Eastern Townships during the fifties and sixties; I am flabbergasted to see how this matter evolved until now. It seems that the "in" thing is not only to tolerate risky practices, but to ensure they subtly become the norm. Hello there! Is everyone feeling well?

Does an honest desire to have safe sex make other people jump?!!! Would it be considered marginal today to respect the health of our genital organs and those of others?

Let me quote Canada's source of information on HIV and hepatitis C:

"*Don't forget that you can also try other safe sexual practices ...*" *(Cf. : www.catie.ca/fr) (in French only)*

Don't forget… Because that is exactly what seems to be happening, we are forgetting the existence of safe sex practices and that sex is not such a horrible activity as long as we know how to do it!! Good manners also seem to have been neglected during sexual activity! For example, at eighteen years old – and oh, so very soon! It's scandalous! Some people are trying to introduce compulsory vaccination against HPV for young girls, as early as fourteen years old – as a young and gentle person, and with all that I know today, I would never ask another person to take medication in order just to be with me!

Young people most definitely face huge challenges and should be kept informed of the ins and outs of having a fulfilling love life.

In the lucrative oral contraceptive market, people have to make medical decisions depending on their medical health and in the absence of adequate references, since circumstances and information pertaining to the numerous synthetic substances are unclear and their actual impact not often taken into account.

Here again, it appears quite evident that gender duality can sometimes provide completely meaningless models. Thus, a pseudo-idealistic young woman – one who accepts to play the role in which she is essentially confined – might find herself seriously targeted to be designated as grand master of copulation activities and the only one to conduct the delicate operations surrounding reproduction and contraception. While a pseudo-idealistic boy – who accepts to play the role in which he is essentially confined, – would have been kept perhaps since birth, in total ignorance of his real sensuality and of the responsible management of his sperm, causing inwardly an immense disruption and distress that would entrap him during the whole of his life.

And while a contraceptive method like the birth control pill for women has been clearly identified as having harmful impacts on their health, the pill for men has been abandoned for those exact same reasons! It's quite intriguing, isn't it?

"What about the pill for men? Research is ongoing in this area... Men will have to wait for a pill that will offer them the protection they want, without the unwanted side-effects."

http://sante.canoe.ca/channel_health_features_details.asp?article_id=524&channel_id=29&health_feature_id=167&relation_id=143
(In French only)

However, there is always the alternative to use other sterilization methods such as tubal ligation, even though it has unwanted side-effects and health risks.

« Risks associated with tubal ligation are generally linked to an adverse reaction to anaesthesia (lung and cardiac problems, etc.), the risk of infection during the operation or complications such as the perforation of the uterus, damaged blood vessels, which happens

in rare cases. If the surgical procedure fails, there is a higher risk of having an ectopic pregnancy.

(Cf.http://www.fqpn.qc.ca/?methodes=ligature-des-trompes)(in French only)

Or a vasectomy with a potential risk for complications due to surgery: infections and bleeding, less than 1%, pressure on the testicle and the discomfort associated with the congestion of the epididymis in less than 5% of the cases, a painful scarred nodule on the canal (granuloma) (around 1%) and very rare chronic pains (around 0,1%). (*Cf. http://www.vasectomie.net/la_vasectomie.htm)(In French only)*

Chapter 31

Ecological Perspective

In this book, I am attempting to put things in a more natural, logical and ecological context, in a way that respects each person's health. I wanted to begin by showing sexuality is a healthy, living and invigorating love, within the boundaries based on the understanding of the human body and its biology.

You may say that this whole text – and I will agree with you on that – is all about a vast topic highly based on science and intelligence, a topic we don't dare talk about out of respect for the readers' pure thoughts, a topic I myself needed time to make my own, and which I wanted to talk to you about, if only by professional conviction. Yes, this book talks about our orifices and one which is the principal vector for parasites, viruses, dangerously contagious diseases from where invasive pathogens are evacuated. The target, responsible for so many ills…: The rectum – and we very well understand why – with so much at stake that this plays a central role in the development of my theory of *Ecological Love.* Others can safely say, that … everything in here revolves around the anus.

Indeed, according to statements made by modern biology, fecal matter is an infectious agent, spreads germs, has been found to be dangerous and should be stayed clear of.

Fecal contamination in bathing waters leads to no-swim advisories, and when minced beef is found to be contaminated in a specific country, it leads to the systematic recall of tons of beef from the food supply chain. And this only happens when the E. coli bacteria has been detected.

So, if public health officials fear the humble presence of certain amounts of fecal contaminants in bathing waters, what about the harmful presence of this same bacteria in today's sexual practices?

"Feces, their elimination and their supervision have a pivotal role in food hygiene as well as hygiene in general. As a human body waste, it can also be a vector of diseases (primarily cholera)".

(Cf.: http://en.wikipedia.org/wiki/Feces)

Since the scientific community knows enough about the dangers associated with fecal matter, it allows us to avoid unhealthy sexual touching capable of provoking severe conditions, like cancer and eventually the death of one or the two sexual partners.

What is truly astonishing is that there are those who promote the legitimacy of anal intercourse… Also, the question burning everyone's lips is why do men choose such an infectious spot in which to put their penis? Yet, we are conditioned to think that the male anatomy leads us to believe that it is absolutely imperative to insert the male organ into an orifice. It would even seem natural and any other behaviour would seem unnatural. As if there wasn't enough room in the atmosphere to accommodate the male organ….and capable of receiving its semen as well!

We are sometimes conditioned to think women are suitable for receiving sperm, somewhat like warehouses, while medical science puts itself in the position of being the great saviour for all of humanity, when it desperately tries to develop a magic bullet to halt conception brought about by depositing the sperm in what I call the hub of fertility!

When the mere knowledge and willingness of two loving and consenting persons can overcome all these ills, the pharmaceutical industry launches itself into a grand rescue operation for the sake of the bewildered lovers and their passionate love-making, and it no doubt wants the semen deposited into the fertile ground. Even though everyone tends to believe that their intimate relationship is unique, how many of them actively try to conform themselves to the prescribed manner, thinking they are quite original and highly personal in their behaviours? These same people will give each other serious diseases, multiple infections, irritations, recurring chlamydia, and so on.

Not knowing what else to do besides penetration to achieve pleasure leads us to imagine the worst when the tendency is to say "Oh, it's unclean, but let's do it anyway!!!" And then, the dirt and bacteria conveniently enter into a young girl's or boy's or intersex person's orifice or urethra and propagate within their pure bodies – which really will not stay in that state for long… –. Once inside, those imprisoned substances will continue, with impunity, to do great harm, for several hours, several days, several weeks or even years, and all that from a single short Friday night encounter, which looks innocent enough, but is sheer desperation.

For example, with regards to prostate cancer versus sexual relationships:

« Marie-Élise Parent and her team can only make "highly speculative" assumptions in an effort to explain this association. "This could come from a greater exposure to STD or it could be that anal penetration can cause a lesion to the prostate," she said cautiously.

(Cf.: http://www.nouvelles.umontreal.ca/recherche/sciences-de-la-sante/20141028-avoir-eu-plusieurs-femmes-dans-sa-vie-reduirait-le-risque-de-cancer-de-la-prostate.html) (in French only)

However, sexual arousal can be managed intelligently and sensibly so as to remain pleasant, before, during and after… (See *Ecological Love: The Practice.*)

To constantly repeat the same gestures imitating those linked to conception would have been unthinkable, were it not for the harsh command to practice a sexuality based exclusively on the reproductive process. We must understand the extent of this obligation, which, once it has been incorporated into the teachings and behaviours as the only right way to act, becomes an integral part of popular thinking and self-regulates by the simple and effective control of individuals so conditioned. Learning certain concepts in order to behave "correctly" in society is in fact part of the socializing process.

We are entitled to question the validity of these teachings and their sources in order to know who are the powers exercising these kinds of controls, where do they come from, and what exactly are they proclaiming? Whose interests do they really serve?

In a time of change towards a planet more environmentally respectful, the fundamental question is to know what the population's specific interest in this matter is.

All of this is not a question of chance, though sometimes we want to believe it is, as if it was another cause instead of our mysterious behaviours coming directly from the cosmos that may be responsible for all our ills, in our stead.

On this issue, we have often seen medicine conclude with the following rhetorical flourish, and hand down its prognosis like a bombshell: "*You have this or that*", but without linking the ill to the cause from which a possible contamination could have taken place inside the body due to the insertion of fecal matters, for example.

Let alone this regressive attitude against excessive penetration responsible for the current overpopulation, which started in the 19th century, and was intensified by war and terror, particularly during both world wars. As if there was a human interest somehow – purely commercial, of course – in surreptitiously introducing shamelessly to the whole world a culture of reproduction followed by mass destruction, and erect it into a system.

Chapter 32

Pure and Simple Love

Oh, of course, pure and simple love is in dire need of recognition! We often mistake its meaning. We wrongly confuse it with platonic love or abstinence. We have the false perception that it does not include pleasure or sexuality.

Yet, after having been quite literally pushed into behaving like everyone else, with surprising harshness I might add, and being quite candid about the management of semen and deferring its responsibility to the field of medicine, well, there you go, it is high time to stand up and speak out!

Oh, my sweet love, and those tender kisses in my neck!

In the words to my song *"In my hand I hold a miracle!.... Nothing will stop me, nothing"*, let us remember that the best love in the world comes from soft, tender and skilled hands. And that we are completely determined to remain pure and to partake in healthy practices!!

Quebec is a special place where experiences in purity and natural health are encouraged. People come from all over the world because they are committed to maintaining harmonious relationships with the environment, thus peaceful relationships with their counterparts.

Nothing will ever attenuate the power of human straightforwardness, particularly in a place where the population is the sovereign power, where there is no barrier to the freedom of speech and action and where everyone's dignity is respected.

But what happens if we observe the presence of groups, among the population, who practice activities contrary to this fundamental principle? If we notice that some people, for example, force their fellow human beings to procreate and that the population is threatened with imprisonment or death if it does not comply with this order? Isn't it our duty as citizens to speak out against these abuses? Yes, absolutely. Especially if it happens in a so-called democratic society, where it is prohibited for anyone to undermine the integrity of another person?

However, we have noticed during our research and analysis activities, the presence of just those kinds of practices, especially among certain groups of individuals who do not respect freedom and who apply coercive pressure on their members in order for the members to give birth, at a rate approaching eight children per couple. There are reports going around that certain groups use the forced reproductive strategy to increase their demographic weight to win political power and establish their dictatorship. And, of course, the pressures exercised over their own increasingly affect all people across the country and even across the entire world.

Yet, having a group living under a separate political regime, within the boundaries of a democratic regime, and adhering to its own civil and criminal code *sui generis* is very alarming. A country cannot have 2 civil codes.

The Civil Code of Quebec, in harmony with the Charter of Rights and Freedoms and the general principles of law, governs persons, relations between persons, and property. It deals with the principal rules relating to human rights, family, estate, property and civil responsibility, obligations, claims and hypothecs, evidence and limitation, etc.

Engaging in malicious interests towards the host society in order to reproduce and thus conquer more space, sparks an outrage among even the best minds. This situation demands for concrete measures to be urgently adopted, in order to counter the political invasion that has been clearly and publicly proclaimed by its authors, and undertaken by them, using oppressive and conquerable methods. It is in fact totally unethical – and urgent in the current state of the world, to condemn this, when overpopulation and human poverty are so prevalent – to provoke a race to populate – to see who would make the most children – with the stated intention of conquering more space.

It is thus critical to form a barrier against this kind of culture controlled by totalitarianism and to object without delay to any enforced pressure specifically coming from written and audiovisual teachings, or others, involving incitement against violence towards those who offend the regime and those who refuse to comply with a degrading sexist mentality.

It is a new kind of war, the war to populate. A hellish strategy which serves everyone's interests, except of course those of human beings procreated in this way, and are, to some extent, the victims forced to obey this diktat and offer their work skills to the dictators… Et voilà…

It's quite absurd that in totalitarian regimes – and admittedly, it was exactly the same in Quebec, namely during my own childhood – that pawns are most likely not allowed to develop any kind of friendship with a same-sex person when it is suspected that feelings of pleasure are present!

In countries under dictatorship rule, who meddle in the lives of their fellow citizens and decide to punish them because they feel joy when coming into contact with human skin, for example? Who sets the limits on feelings? How does friendship differ from sensual friendship?

If you feel happiness for one minute and an increase in your libido…Is it homosexuality? Are the changes in your libido linked or not to your friendship? They are difficult questions to ask, and even harder to answer. But be careful, when facing such tremendous punishment, the answer is decisive… Hey, it's a question of life or death in certain countries! And the terrible thing about these political systems is that too often their tormenters act according to their own ideas instead of those put forward by the accused. For that, they risk terrible punishment before having had any time to give their opinion, express their candour or claim their innocence.

It is a well known fact, that the despicable rules surrounding the legendary sexuality of certain dictators and their habits of piercing or perforating someone, and so on, have oppressed more than one slave. This is why we must respond urgently to these internationally unacceptable realities.

And is it possible to even imagine that one day, those who practice such horrific activities can be "touched" by divine grace, and finally acquire a generous heart and the desire for a pure, simple and ecological freedom!

On a more positive note, this truly fantastic movement we are currently witnessing completely redeems our sensuality. It praises the true virtues of the freedom of our sensuality. We are breaking the bonds that have held us captive under an unbearable stranglehold when we constantly had to start over again, when from the time we became adults it was our turn to repeat the act of procreation. That is the mandate that was asked of future generations, when the church, clearly allied to the state, wanted everyone to make *"children who make children, who make children, who make children... (Cf. Theatre play: "Trois et Sept Le Numéro Magique 1977 (in French only)*

But the devasting consequences, poverty, child neglect and violence that have now been acknowledged as horrendous disasters, have the international bodies scrambling to put a stop to it in the form of valiant actions they constantly repeat, but to no avail.

How can we possibly expect responsible parenting when people, knee-deep in poverty, and by a stroke of bad luck, become parents by force? And right away, fearful people will call this fact into question by saying *"Of course not, we choose to be parents..."* So, let's agree, that this is not necessarily true in all cases.

First of all, let us consider the testimony of persons who have suffered from this and not the ones that have succeeded.

How many of us feel they are supernumeraries? This is another important question – and will be the subject of another forthcoming book: *The Supernumeraries* –.

"Nearly half the world's inhabitants, 2.8 billion people, do not have the means to feed, educate, house or care for themselves." (Cf. : Article de Louis Maurin, La misère du monde Alternatives Économiques n° 177 - janvier 2000)(in French only)

What is freedom of choice worth in our modern societies if there is no strong alternative? Between being berated and being admired much like what we vow to our parents, should we hesitate regarding its future? The path is all laid for us. From childhood to adolescence, the names qualifying friendship between same-sex persons are literally despicable. You don't even have to set foot outside the house that you are routinely labelled a homosexual as if it was the worst possible crime.

Therefore, it is not surprising that as soon as you have the chance you want to form an opposite sex couple. And given the fusional and deep nature of a relationship centred on reproduction, conception-contraception, and also given the fact that birth control pills can only be taken for a limited time, often only for a three year period, one must admit that it is practically inevitable, after a few years, to choose parenthood. In fact young people have no alternative but to start a family, once the period of taking contraceptive pills has elapsed. For all intents and purposes this is not free choice as there is only one possibility. There is no second option – short of undergoing a permanent operation –. And what about those who become pregnant while claiming that is not what they wanted, or those who claim their method of birth control failed. Or yet again, what about the ones terrorized at the idea of fatherhood and having to hide it?

Would it not have been better to remain in the realm of sensuous respect instead of falling into fusional and conceptional genital relationships, since often, in these cases, neither partner had the intention to procreate, but rather had only hoped to experience pleasure…And we all agree, that since the issue of pleasure is such a taboo topic, information about it is rather rare…

How many human beings have no other choice but to live under the yoke of this oppression? It stands to reason that the proliferation of "surplus human beings" – and they would not have been created were it not for this diktat – has terrible consequences on the incidence of poverty and violence. Let's say in this case that it's easy enough to link cause and effect. The search for individual well-being is totally destroyed by the diktat's rigid stance and seems to benefit only the interests of a very small number of super-rich individuals.

Sure enough, we can conclude that the accumulation of goods is useful to the scientific and technological evolution, but on the other hand, we also have the power to take into account, along with these progresses, the well-being of individuals and societies, and correct the speed with which these activities take place as is presently the case within movements advocating to slowdown its pace on several levels.

Naturally, certain individuals are very very happy with their family life project and as far as they are concerned the child is the most amazing event in the universe!!! Of course! But please, leave those who wish to abstain, in peace! They know what they are doing.

We can trust each other to make the right decisions without any undue pressure.

Multinationals love chaste young women and men, for which plans have been made for them to go to school, so they can land fascinating and good paying jobs.

However, not every child is necessarily comfortable with this type of life and sometimes even with his or her own condition. If they wish to wear clothes or other items that don't correspond to those generally assigned to their genders, they will have terrible problems throughout their lives. Is this the gift we want to give our offsprings?

Since the context is such a difficult one, before giving birth to a child wouldn't it be more desirable if the offer was friendlier? Of course it is our duty, as creatures of nature, to try and better monitor our desires and actions and connect them to our real interests.

In fact no person can reap any benefits from such a wrongful command applied with such viciousness and madness than the one concerning imposed coupling.

UN studies and others on demographic prospects increasingly show a potential slowdown of the staggering population growth. Even a decrease in population growth is a valid solution to endemic human poverty problems. The first hurdle to cross is without a doubt to begin a global dialogue which will generate hope for the freedom to live and the freedom to love.

"During the International Conference on Population in Cairo, Egypt, in 1994, the United Nations rapporteurs had hoped to

promote the right of women to decide for themselves the number of children they wanted to have. But the plea in favour of women's emancipation faced strong resistance."

(Cf.http://www.larousse.fr/encyclopedie/divers/population_mondiale_sept_milliards_dhommes/185885)(in French only)

Although today, the humanist movement gives us the opportunity to speak more freely about the rights of women, men and intersex persons to decide for themselves if they want to procreate.

"It is not possible to speak of economic development without referencing one of its key components: demography. In an essay that he has just published, Dr. Jack A. Goldstone, with scathing relevancy, summarizes the key concerns of a constantly changing world, severely underestimated up to now. He recalls that only forty years ago, Paul Enrlich, a biologist, issued a warning that really impressed people. He wrote that at its present rate, the human population explosion will lead to mass hunger beginning in the seventies.

While the planet faces a drastic drop in the production of essential consumer goods, the World Wide Fund for Nature (formally the World Wildlife Fund) published on October 29th 2008, the "Living Planet Report 2008".

According to this report, more than three quarters of the world's population live in nations that are ecological debtors – their consumption has outstripped their country's biocapacity (expressed as the "ecological footprint"). The authors are seeking a "reduction in population, individual consumption and resources used, or wastes emitted, to produce goods and services".

The criterion "ecological footprint", used by the WWF was developed by a British Foundation, Optimum Population Trust, that campaigned openly to reduce world population by two-thirds and bring it down to two or three billion people."

(Cf. Source : Solidarité et Progrès - 04.11.08 (in French only)
http://www.geopopulation.com/20081106/selon-wwf-il-faut-reduire-de-deux-tiers-la-population-mondiale/) (in French only)

"Since the Cro-Magnon man, it took 40 000 years to reach 2.5 billion people. It took 37 years for the global population to double its size between 1950 and 1986, from 2.5 to 5 billion inhabitants and only 23 years for it to grow nearly as much and reach 7 billions inhabitants in 2011.

(Cf.http://www.larousse.fr/encyclopedie/divers/population_mondiale__sept_milliards_dhommes/185885)(in French only)

A large part of people the world over have to live with the very difficult consequences of a non organic conception due to inappropriate pressures, and their testimonies express their misery and the difficulties they face trying to integrate and adapt themselves. The current situation is totally untenable.

Ecological Love is pure, simple, healthy, and easy, it embodies an ideal organic conception as well as the practice of an idyllic sensuality.

It does not require anti-stress gadgets due to risky practices. And the joy it brings is in itself a peaceful and truthful place. Neither party is obliged to be anything but true to themselves. The genitals are accepted in all their uniqueness, and practices are dependent upon each partner's distinct characteristics.

Is it a question of ignoring the reality of fertility, as if it did not exist, while doing our best – methods of birth control are never 100% effective – to be infertile using carcinogenic agents? This situation, while quite common, creates an ambiance in which a man's sperm looses its purpose and becomes a simple gelatinous substance, while his partner takes on the entire responsibility, and then everything happens just like the clips, films and video games, etc., so skillfully capture. In each case, the woman is compelled – under the influence of the pharmaceutical industry – to lie to herself, while pretending to have the power to practice conception, and escape it at the same time, all the while being impacted by negative side effects like weight gain, bleeding, migraines, sore breasts, reduced libido… (*Cf.* http://www.aufeminin.com/info-contraception-pillule-contraceptive.html*)* (in French only)

Acting as if nothing is happening, while doing the exact opposite… Meanwhile, the male partner is left out and becomes somewhat unimportant, becomes mired in ignorance and nonchalance, and thus adopts an uneducated and disengaged attitude that can rope him in and unwittingly derail him towards disrespect.

However, we should acknowledge that not everyone wants to play this underhand game. The truth of the matter is it only succeeds in generating huge profits for already booming industries that produce synthetic pills.

Fortunately the percentage of people moving away from this model is increasing considerably, as they do not identify with this kind of mixup.

And while others choose to believe that the particular shape of the man justifies the fact that he must absolutely enter his sex somewhere, others argue that the phallic shape is free, unique and complete and that there is absolutely no need for it to be introduced into another shape. Take for example a blade of grass; did nature give it an opening in which to enter? Water from a faucet flows freely, without having to be introduced into another shape. Do men have to enter their penis somewhere in order to urinate, walk, walk backwards, jump or dive?

Why do we think nature forces the reproductive organ to penetrate and even, on some occasion, enter any orifice it finds in its way, without even acknowledging its vulnerability and its strength as well? Isn't his organ free? Isn't he capable of ejaculating into the air!! Isn't the surrounding air infinite and attractive enough to him? Numerous individuals have expressed their views and are happy to be free to behave with finesse and intelligence in a country precisely like Canada.

As well, among people of all ages – often, and against all prejudice among gay people – there is a complete refusal to be confined into already defined roles as well as a destiny mapped out since birth, according to rules which do not at all correspond to their more authentic values. And these people do not invade each other, but simply favour healthier and more respectful relationships.

If certain persons have a genuine willingness to procreate at a given moment, there have always existed a number of ways to create new life including the one where sperm is carefully deposited on the thigh and with extreme delicacy finds its way to the ova.

Yet, there is no need whatsoever to deposit the sperm at the back of the throat, is there? Women's orifices are delicate. To find the vaginal entrance, one could think that it would probably be advisable to wear a headlamp and carry a magnifying glass in order not to land into the neighbouring orifices.

There is no need to force the entrance in an effort to deposit the sperm all the way to the cervix. It finds its own way. That is well known and has been proven. Yes, there are people fascinated by the inside of the body and they just love to touch internal organs during vaginal or anal penetration with their hands, fingers, wrists, arms, tongue, etc., etc., Their pleasure is detailed in a number of texts. That's true. But the pleasure gained by taking such health risks is really more stressful than inspiring when someone values health. And the danger, nowadays, is to observe how these practices have been formally endorsed, whereas gentler and external sexual practices have been unfairly infantilized.

Better documentation is needed on the highly pleasurable and aphrodisiac effects of certain verbal exchanges, looks, tender kisses in the neck, behind the ears, hugs, and body touching by loving hands, and all of this without coming into contact with mucus or saliva, in a context of mutual attraction and scrupulous respect and where communication remains honest and respectful.

For some people this can prove to be the height of pleasure and this type of sexual practice can be their greatest fantasy. Yet, this pure vision is the constant target of painful mockery in numerous households…Even though it has been so beautifully touched upon in poems and songs of well-known artists:

"But infinite love will mount in my soul." (Cf.: Arthur Rimbaud, Sensation, Poem, March 1870.)

Even though asexuality has been largely symbolized in the arts, this is not the issue here, as I am sure you have understood we are not talking about abstinence or avoidance. However, we do consider it completely normal and legitimate to have beneficial periods of solitudes, rest, retreat or abstinence.

Thankfully, with *Ecological Love*, the young generation slowly begins to taste the pleasures of the flesh with the greatest of joy – minus the stress – and this spiritual revolution exempts them from obligation to practice a sexuality frought with dangerous and inadmissible behaviours.

Conclusion

The desire for emancipation undoubtedly stems from the fear of being enslaved by certain human powers and their corresponding threats. In the face of dictatorship, the emancipation process is really happening because of the slow rise of a more participatory democracy in Europe and America, where no one is allowed to undermine the life of their fellow human beings by ordering them to obey a set of rules which in no way corresponds to the demands of their own freedom.

My sound mind can no longer withstand any offence to the expression of justice, and my professional conscience as a sociologist has inevitably lead me to speak out about the lack of respect in the integrity of each human being which in turn has enabled me to present the result of a research – that has lasted thirty-five years, day after day – conducted in the most rigorous way possible, with the ultimate goal of unlocking the layers of socio-economic and political intrigues hitting our societies head-on and horrifying those who favour humanism, and the meeting of two worlds bogged down in a quagmire: democracy versus theocracy and their respective civil and criminal codes.

These investigations have brought to light details on the causes and motivations behind the cruelest commands our era has ever seen as well as the most untenable atrocities, enough to make any defender of human rights on the planet, shudder.

I have lived in a country where everyone has proudly participated in the clearing of lands with vigor and determination. We have held water, taken from the streams in our hands with the utmost respect for nature and universal life.

As well, when the time came to consider the issue of gender-related concepts and encourage each other to put forward the best practices in terms of human relationships, we were pleased with the fact that only a few small details would have to be adjusted. Actual demands are the recognition of the gender-related triad and the acknowledgement of efforts made in favour of destigmatization.

In order to improve ourselves, it is extremely important to continue discussing, in complete safety, the issues that are most relevant, to hear everyone's complaints and to promote the emergence of reliable solutions, with the solidarity it deserves.

In the last century, it is worthwhile to note the contribution of Eleanor Roosevelt, First Lady of the United States from 1933 to 1945 as President of the Drafting Commission of the Universal Declaration of Human Rights, diplomat and activist.

She circled the globe with the Universal Declaration of Human Rights – adopted by the General Assembly of the United Nations, in 1948 – following the unimaginable atrocities that took place during the Second World War, and in which it was agreed by the signatories that the horrific scenes they had observed went beyond all limits.

In fact, it was the shock of seeing bleeding bodies, sometimes completely dismembered, that made no sense at all. The complete absurdity of these frightful events soon became apparent.

Thus, out of such evilness resulting from the destruction of lives and places, was born a clear vision of the future where conflicts would be settled through oral communication. This global project was extremely well received. What a wonderful idea this was to show zero tolerance in the face of serious material damages resulting from human conflict!

When we look at the situation from a galactic perspective, indeed, the self-destruction of the earth seems to be completely illogical. And, as every conflict is resolved by identifying its roots, I have attempted, in this essay, to point the finger at the primary basis for human wrangling. And it became clear, that the reason which justifies the failure to respect human rights is the acquisition and distribution of wealth.

What is ultimately at stake here is the effective sharing of wealth on the basis of the number of beneficiaries. And although wealth increases with the number of workers and provides added value to nature's products, profit-sharing is still disproportionate.

We had to find out why profit-sharing represented so little for some and so much for others. Why was there so little empathy on the part of those who possess great wealth towards certain other people?

In fact the question becomes more complicated when we try to find out why the love of some does not reach others. How can we feel such contempt for people who are related to us by blood, when we leave them deprived of their basis needs? Because one way or another we are all linked by the bonds of blood.

The question is not that wealth belongs to one person or another, but rather if that person or the other is able to share the goods of the earth that have been entrusted to them. Are they able to fulfill the dreams of others besides themselves, and create jobs for them?

It is well known, resources are shared only in very small and unjust proportions. Worst still, wealth is transformed into currency and almost entirely remains in the form of currency where it is exchanged at a subterranean level, without ever surfacing nor ever becoming involved in the creation and financing of projects, to earn more money, yes, but also creating projects financially-geared toward communities, where profits are really used to expand human well-being.

Now we are at the heart of the problem. Why give birth to children who will never have access to basic necessities? But what are those basic necessities? This is another issue to be discussed in a forthcoming volume: *The Essentials.*

The importance of the *Ecological Love* concept is based on the the acuteness of our judgement, inspired by a universal energy and which in turn is quite adequate to garantee that beings brought into this world will be blessed and cherished by life.

However, in many countries around the world, this area is completely ignored while each human being's judgement concerning their own reproduction is crucial.

Furthermore, it appears that the greatest source of violence existing on Earth at present comes from the diktat imposed on reproduction, as well as on the population's sexuality.

We are all subjected to the same obligation, to commit only to sensual practices for the purpose of reproduction under penalty of rejection, but, even worse, of death, imprisonment, stoning, and many more. And you've only got to look at the very virulence of these attacks against friendly encounters by same-sex individuals, to see how fundamentally opposed are the dictates about homosexuality in free countries as well as in countries under dictatorship.

It is therefore urgent that we restore the *Ecological Love,* a pure and simple relationship so as to totally do away with the shadow of violence.

Regarding this issue, we also should mention the huge success non sexist teaching methods have had in our democratic countries.

In Quebec, since the seventies, we can attest to the birth of more egalitarian human interactions and the great advent of couples and individuals who practice *Ecological Love,* where organic reproduction is respected and the development of a healthy sensuality has succeeded in establishing a safe and peaceful climate for sharing.

I would like to congratulate the people of Quebec for having established a climate of freedom in our democratic political system, our civil and criminal codes, in a territory where winter conditions are harsh and where everyone is so brave, vigorous, so beautiful and so real.

And I have no doubt that our legendary strenght and authenticity will rise to the occasion to ensure we safeguard these incomparable gains.

With this aim in mind, it seems imperative that we agree on the following: "Forced reproduction is a crime against humanity."

Sociology examines, among other things, the way societies transmit values to their members. In this way, through education, important values and legal advice are transmitted.

Written and audiovisual teaching materials sometimes will show us, in a more insidious fashion, how to behave according to models that correspond to stereotyped images so that we act either as a woman or as a man, and subsequently how we act towards each other.

To Simone de Beauvoir's famous saying "One is not born, but rather becomes a woman", I would add that the proposed models do not actually correspond to the trinitarian gender differences, in that our learned behaviours are not harmonized with each person's natural tendencies.

When one questions these teachings and representations, we realize how much the relationship between same-sex people is prohibited in many documents coming from too many countries around the world. And we certainly understand, without a doubt, that while we live our own – hard won – experience of freedom, we remain vulnerable to the violent threats made by dictatorships on enforced reproduction.

We can certainly dream of a more joyful reality for every person alive. But…

Land and soil erosion, overuse of natural resources, increase of contaminants, the rise of inconveniences brought on by the non-peaceful cohabitation of taxpayers. Human beings held hostage and enslaved by masters they know are not in their right minds.

War and destruction. Discomfort among inhabitants. Anger among the targeted populations. For both the people and the scientific breakthroughs, research is extremely biased and technologies are geared toward commercial interests and are developed in isolation.

...It is a large part of the people's quality of life on the planet that is severely deteriorating.

However, since in a democracy, sovereign power lies with the people – it is a must – we need to express our will to keep on experiencing freedom and improving our living conditions by actively seeking out our personal and common interests and refusing to submit ourselves to the diktat which forces us into strict roles.

Women, men and intersex persons have the power to maintain

peace by associating together in order to express their unswerving devotion to the ecological characteristics of Love and to relationships in general.

The endearment to *Ecological Love* is the result of relationships between human beings where the safety and respect of their bodies are recognized as being essential rights and play an active and ecological role in improving the living conditions on Earth: it is our duty as human beings.

www.ingramcontent.com/pod-product-compliance
Ingram Content Group UK Ltd.
Pitfield, Milton Keynes, MK11 3LW, UK
UKHW041940190726
13854UKWH00004B/1695